Customer Message Management

Increasing Marketing's Impact on Selling

Tim Riesterer and Diane Emo

Australia • Brazil • Japan • Korea • Mexico • Singapore • Spain • United Kingdom • United States

CENGAGE
Learning™

Customer Message Management:
Increasing Marketing's Impact on
Selling
Tim Riesterer and Diane Emo

Composed by: Interactive Composition
Corporation

Printed in the United States of America
by RR Donnelly—Crawfordsville

© 2006 Cengage Learning

This publication is designed to provide accurate and authoritative information in regard to the subject matter covered. It is sold with the understanding that the publisher is not engaged in rendering legal, accounting, or other professional services. If expert assistance is required, the services of a competent professional person should be sought.

For product information and technology assistance,
contact us at
Cengage Learning Customer & Sales Support,
800-354-9706.
For permission to use material from this text or product,
submit all requests online at
www.cengage.com/permissions.
Further permissions questions can be emailed to
permissionrequest@cengage.com.

Library of Congress Cataloging in Publication Number is available. See page 178 for details.

ISBN-13: 978-0-324-31316-1
ISBN-10: 0-324-31316-0

Cengage Learning
5191 Natorp Boulevard
Mason, Ohio 45040
USA

This book is printed on acid-free paper.
5 6 7 12 11 10

CONTENTS

ACKNOWLEDGEMENTS

We've often said that the topic of increasing marketing's impact on sales is more of a professional mission than a job for us. We've spent our time on the mission field pinpointing the disconnects between sales and marketing, aligning the two functions to work more closely together, and most importantly, doing the hard work of developing and implementing a structured, repeatable process to help companies do this "on purpose" instead of "by accident."

The Customer Message Management (CMM) processes and tools are being implemented with a growing roster of progressive companies. We are grateful for these visionary organizations, especially our fearless champions inside who are willing to stand in the gap between marketing and sales—and *do things differently*. Thanks to them, we are able to share a step-by-step approach for impacting revenue generation in a sustainable, unified and meaningful way.

Thank you:

- Dennis Dunlap, CEO of the American Marketing Association, for believing in the category of sales and marketing integration— investing the full support of the AMA to help develop the principles of CMM, and co-sponsoring the Customer Message Management Leadership Forum since 2002.
- Mike Bosworth, customer-centric, solution-selling guru, for helping us make sure that whatever we're telling marketing people will work for real sales people.
- Bob Schmonsees, marketing and sales disconnect visionary, for seeing the "black hole" and setting the stage for CMM with his great book.
- Jim Dickie and Barry Trailer, keepers of the best sales effectiveness data, for connecting the dots between CMM and sales impact.
- Dave Sutton, enterprise marketing management leader, for his willingness to share ideas, advice and business ideas.
- Adria Clawson, the world's most spectacular copywriter, for helping bring our CMM tools and templates to life.

While this book and our professional mission to integrate marketing and sales are good things, we want to thank our spouses—Laura and Rob—who keep us focused on life's mission and the best things: God, family, and sports.

Tim Riesterer and Diane Emo

SECTION ONE

CMM IN PRINCIPLE: AN EXECUTIVE OVERVIEW

CHAPTER 1

WHAT IS CUSTOMER MESSAGE MANAGEMENT?

What is this book about, and how can you use it to your benefit? The focus of *Customer Message Management* is helping individuals and organizations increase marketing and sales effectiveness by focusing on the last hope for competitive differentiation—your customer messaging.

Specifically, we seek to help companies in five key areas:

1. Create a sense of value for customers.
2. Elevate the company from selling products (services) to solutions.
3. Create and deliver more relevant and compelling messaging.
4. Cast a consistent "single voice" to the customer across all selling touch-points.
5. Improve the performance of B and C reps and channel partners.

Doing this successfully demands that marketing and sales come out of their neutral corners and rally to the cause of *improving the customer conversation.* We believe that mending the traditional disconnect between these two groups and focusing everyone's energy where it belongs requires a new corporate discipline called *Customer Message Management.*

Customer Message Management is a cross-functional approach between marketing and sales to *create* better brand, marketing, and selling messages based on customer business roles and goals; *deliver* those messages across all selling touch-points in a way that can be personalized for each prospect and customer interaction; and *equip* more consistent and consultative sales cycles.

The ideas, principles, and practices in this book are the result of the last five years of development and field testing with world-class companies and market leaders such as American Express, Federal Express, Caterpillar, Unisys, AmerisourceBergen, SAS Institute, ADP, HP, Manpower, ITW, Experian, Oce Printing Systems, and others.

It's All About the Customer Conversation

Our company, the CMM Group, has been fortunate enough to partner with the American Marketing Association, the CMO Council, CSO Insights, and various corporate sponsors to create the Customer Message Management

Forum (www.cmmforum.com), an industry consortium with the express purpose to help increase marketing's impact on sales effectiveness.

The Customer Message Management Forum started as a group of sales and marketing experts and thought leaders who wanted to repair the disconnect between their two functions. Our objective was to begin building best practices for working better together to improve companies' selling success.

Improving the "customer conversation" emerged as the key missing link. In today's highly competitive and perceived parity markets, it's not *what* you sell but *how* you sell that matters. The sales experts said, "It's not about where I show up (a specific reference to marketing leads); it's about what I say when I get there that really counts."

The customer conversation, *and the customer messaging behind it,* has become the last bastion of competitive differentiation. We believe that the marketer's most powerful—but often overlooked—branding tool is the quality of the sales cycle itself. Driving the brand from the company headquarters level down through its sales reps and various channels is what separates great brands from also-rans. That's exactly where companies should focus their efforts in their search for competitive differentiation.

Customer Message Management promises to help companies transform their 30,000-foot brand promises and marketing positioning into more consistent and compelling selling messages used in the 3.5-foot customer-buying conversation. By providing practical examples of how companies can push their brand messaging further "downstream," CMM helps marketers have a more relevant and serious impact on revenue-generating activities. And salespeople get the messaging and tools that truly support a consultative sales cycle.

This book is designed to help educate and train you on the Customer Message Management approach. We will help you create and deliver sales-ready messaging and support to drive these all-important customer conversations.

There's a sense of urgency around solving this problem. That's why we will present concepts and tools that can be applied immediately to improve the consistency and quality of your company's customer messaging and impact your next quarter results.

The Five Pressing Issues That Customer Message Management Solves

Customer Message Management is designed to solve the five most pressing issues marketing and sales executives want to solve when it comes to increasing selling effectiveness. As you read these descriptions, imagine where you and your company might be struggling, and begin to prioritize the key areas that you want to change.

1. Create a Sense of Value for Customers.

The amount of business information that your customers must sift through to make business decisions doubles every 1,100 days[1]. Picture them culling through mountains of detailed content to make a decision. It's no wonder they have a hard time differentiating your subtle and esoteric product feature arguments from those of your competitors.

Your Challenges:

- Ensure everyone in your company shares a common understanding of what constitutes a differentiated value proposition.
- Establish a shared structure and approach for creating value propositions that can be used in the field to distinguish your company, and help customers see the value of your solutions.
- Develop value propositions in the customer's context (their goals, needs, problems), not in your company or product context, to help create value for the customer instead of inferring benefits from features and functions.

How CMM Can Help   Avoiding parity in your value propositions and providing clarity from the clutter means moving beyond traditional product-based features and benefits. CMM's *Value Creation*™ process can give you a much-needed strategic corporate discipline for creating value propositions within the context of the customer profile, business needs, and desired business impact.

2. Elevate from Selling Products to Solutions.

Product-based messaging isn't working. Customers care less about what "it" does, and more about how they can solve a business problem by using "it." Customer want to solve a problem, meet a need, or achieve a goal. Your

---

[1] Bill Jensen, *Simplicity: The New Competitive Advantage in a World of More, Better, Faster.* New York: Perseus Books, 2001, page 23.

products are not a "solution" until a prospect or customer says so. And they can't say it if you don't help them envision themselves applying it to successfully solve the problem, meet the need, or achieve the goal.

Your Challenges:

- Establish and reinforce a consultative, solution-selling sales approach that continues to work long after your sales training investment "wears off."
- Break down the walls between organizational "product silos" that prevent you from developing an integrated solution to customer problems.
- Move from the mindset that solutions are just longer lists of product features and services to an organizational discipline that demonstrates response to customer needs.

How CMM Can Help Creating a truly customer-focused marketing and sales approach requires that you proactively identify your target customers' key business drivers, and then map your corresponding capabilities as a "best answer" to solving those needs. CMM's *Solution Mapping*™ process helps marketing and sales systematically construct solution scenarios for target customers based on their real-world business needs—and then connect your most appropriate capabilities to build a solution from the customer's perspective.

3. Build Compelling, Relevant Messages into Marketing Campaigns and Collaterals.

The CMM Forum surveys indicate that up to 90 percent of content created for sales support is unused in the field, and that over 97 percent of campaigns are irrelevant to the customers they were intended to attract. This can add up to millions in wasted investment and obviously does little to set you apart in a highly competitive marketplace.

Your Challenges:

- Make sure everyone in marketing knows what an ideal sales cycle and customer buying process look like.
- Determine exactly which messages, tools, and support are needed to sell more effectively in a best-practice sales cycle.

- Transform 30,000-foot headquarters' "marketing speak" into useful, accessible sales conversations, presentations, and documentation that work at the 3.5-foot level.

How CMM Can Help   Creating more effective campaigns and support tools demands better alignment between the consultative conversations that customers want to have, and the way your salespeople talk to them. CMM's *Sales-Cycle-Relevant Marketing*™ process trains you to synch up message development and deployment (marketing communications) with the customer buying process and solution selling approach for bigger impact and business results.

4. Create "One Voice" to the Customer Across Multiple Selling Touch-Points.

The number of departments and people inside companies who create customer messages seems to be growing, as does the number of channels to deliver that content. Conflicting themes, approaches, and one-off, self-styled communications have companies competing with themselves to deliver a coherent story.

Your Challenges:

- Get all internal product, marketing, and sales activities on the same page regarding roles and responsibilities for communicating to the marketplace or customer base.
- Identify the "meaningful interactions" throughout the customer life cycle, and the key "moments of truth" that require messages and support to move the sale forward.
- Establish a consistent message creation and delivery process to build more consistency and high-quality messages for the company, regardless of touch-points or skill levels.

How CMM Can Help   Driving consistency throughout a customer experience is critical. Each interaction should build on the other to a crescendo and ultimate conclusion—that your company and solution best answer their business needs. CMM's *Message Map*™ process creates a consistent corporate discipline for structuring the unstructured customer messaging process and closing the gap between headquarters, the field, and the customer.

5. Increase Performance of B and C Reps and Channel Partners.

Only 10 percent of your sales reps are "A" players, according to statistics promoted by popular sales training programs. Since those top reps already exceed quota, your best opportunity for sales growth is improving the performance of the other 90 percent of reps. In the case of channel partners, they often succeed on your behalf despite your actions! Making sure that all channels can properly articulate your solution is a practical, effective way to gain mindshare and improve performance in support of your sales compensation plan.

Your Challenges:

- Help salespeople have situational conversations and ask consultative questions instead of resorting to a presentation of company facts and product features.
- More effectively target business decision makers—the people who can buy—instead of users; inspire credibility and confidence in your ability to solve their business problems.
- Develop a solution across the product portfolio to create better answers and bigger deals; express real business wins versus contorting generic benefits as "value."

How CMM Can Help Clone the approach, conversations, and competencies that enable "A" reps to construct solutions in response to customer needs. CMM's *Conversation Roadmap*™ process proactively prescribes and populates discussion talk tracks and sales-relevant tools that prepare or coach salespeople to have high-quality customer conversations, presentations, and documentation. Most career salespeople were trained on some form of consultative, solution selling; however, getting trained on an approach without having the message to tell is like having a race car with no fuel. It just won't go.

Key Chapter Take-Aways

- It's not what you sell, but **how you sell that matters.** Also, it's not where your salespeople show up or how you touch the customer but what gets said that makes the difference. The customer conversation is the last bastion of competitive differentiation.

- Customers don't care about your company value proposition; they care about solving problems and getting work done. Product messages miss the mark because they are **too much information too early,** and they leave it to the customer to assemble your value story. Can we leave these critical connections to chance?
- The wedge between sales and marketing comes down to a **fundamental lack of process alignment around the customer buying process**—how customers buy, how sales move forward, who or what communicates to the customer, using which messages to address customer needs.
- Most career salespeople were trained on a sales methodology, but when they turn to their arsenal of sales messages and tools, it doesn't match up. If they want to sell consultatively, they have to **piece messages together, or make them up.**

The next chapter dives deeper into why the sales and marketing disconnect is a drain on your budget and a dilution of your company brand.

CHAPTER 2

IS MARKETING AT RISK OF IRRELEVANCE TO SALES?

This chapter is about relevance. How relevant is your marketing operation to sales success? The content is designed for those of you who are sorting through your roles and responsibilities when it comes to impacting your company's revenue-generating activities. It's also for those of you who want ammunition to get your organization on the same page. Maybe you know what needs to happen, but you need to prove it to someone else to get Customer Message Management on the executive radar.

The marketing and sales disconnect has reached a day of reckoning. Everyone is looking to do more with less, and demonstrate impact for investment. Executive management demands that sales deliver big revenue impact, and requires that marketing do whatever it takes to help them hit the forecast.

But what's it going to take? Something has to give.

The total cost of marketing and sales demands that corporate management take their effectiveness very seriously. There are several rules of thumb for marketing and sales spend: 4–5 percent of operating expenses, 3 percent of total operating budget, 1 percent of assets, 1.5–4 percent of gross income—higher for consumer marketing. Whether B2B or B2C, we're talking about big-budget line items.

Customer acquisition costs are still rising. Competitors are closer than ever. Sales cycles are getting longer. Closing or conversion rates are decreasing. Customer touch-points and channels are proliferating. Do more, more, more with less, less, less.

Here's the dilemma. Marketing departments feature some of the brightest and most educated thinkers in the enterprise. And sales groups contain some of the most passionate and devoted champions in the company. Yet we still struggle to consistently create and communicate the value of our solutions to prospects and customers in a way that drives more revenue.

Marketing feels its efforts to build consistent brand messaging are foiled by salespeople pressing for the next deal, while salespeople view marketing's support as ineffective and unhelpful.

Have you heard any of this around the office?

Marketing Says:

- "Salespeople ignore corporate branding and positioning and do their own thing."
- "We generate leads and create sales support materials that don't get used."
- "We don't know what collateral works or what is being used."
- "We are swamped with one-off sales requests for ad hoc support."
- "Sales is slow to push new products—getting them up to speed takes too long."

Sales Responds:

- "The one-size-fits-all corporate message doesn't help me close orders."
- "Marketing wouldn't know a qualified lead if it tripped on one."
- "We can't find the sales support materials we need when we need them."
- "The sales materials they give us don't fit the way we really sell."
- "Marketing ignores our pleas for help."

Budget Bullseye

There was a cartoon from a few years back that portrays two deer talking with each other. One buck shows the other a target-style design on his chest—complete with bullseye. And the other buck says, "Gee, that's a bummer of a birthmark." We think there's an interesting parallel between the bullseye buck and marketers who are bummed when senior management places a bullesye on their budgets—and they can't show an impact on revenue generation.

The following statistics were generated by the Customer Message Management Forum (www.cmmforum.com) and demonstrate the urgent need for companies to transform their marketing efforts in order to demonstrate more ROI. Because with results like these, it's only a matter of time before marketing is sporting a bullseye target—on its budget.

ROI Goodbye:

- **Up to 90 percent of the marketing messages and materials created for sales support is unused,** or is used inappropriately. This translates to millions of dollars of wasted marketing and communications investment that aren't having a tangible impact on sales effectiveness.

- **Reps spend 40–60 hours a month of valuable customer face time on non-selling activities** related to trying to find, get, and use marketing messages to support specific sales opportunities.
- **Nearly 100 percent of reps are creating and recreating content and deliverables,** which ultimately wind up representing your company deep into the sales cycle creating problems in consistency, accuracy, and appropriateness of the material presented.
- **Only 10 percent of reps do a good job at creating customer messages,** leading to ineffective presentations, poor brand equity, and lower close rates.

One Fortune 50 company completed a Six Sigma study on sales productivity and discovered that its salespeople were spending too much time searching for the right follow-up information and creating their own sales collaterals. This is no surprise. A 2004 CMO Council study[1] showed that "as much as 40% of a typical sales rep's time can be spent in pre- and post-selling activities creating presentations, customizing messaging, and getting ready to engage the customer. Much of this work is repetitive, and takes away from the most valued activity—time with the customer."

So is it a sales problem, or a marketing problem—or both?

The VP of Sales at that Fortune 50 company told us that he estimated his sales time drain to be a $20 million-a-month problem in reduced sales productivity, lost prospect opportunities, and wasted marketing investments. When we asked the VP of marketing what he thought of the situation, he said, "I don't have a problem here . . . we don't go that far downstream. It's a sales problem."

Anyone up for target practice? Within three months the VP of Sales was promoted higher into the Fortune 50 company, and the VP of marketing was out the door. So, who's wearing the bullseye these days?

Irrelevance to your company's selling success is potentially the biggest threat to marketing management today. It's been said, "It's easier to recover from bankruptcy than irrelevancy." So we need to do all we can to avoid it.

---

[1]The CMO Council Survey, "Message Maps and Gaps," sponsored by Sales and Marketing Management and the CMM Forum, June 2004.

Sales Conversations Are Your #1 Branding Tool

We hope you agree that the marketing executive's answer was unacceptable in the example from the previous page. How long would that attitude hold up to a scrutinizing CEO who wants to know how marketing is contributing to the revenue-generating activities of the company?

Whether you like it or not, your company's success rests literally on the shoulders of your sales and services people. It's called their "head"—more specifically their mouth, lips, and tongue. Because what gets said by your reps or through your channels in the sales process is often what makes the difference between getting the meeting or not; making a connection to a customer's business need or missing the mark; establishing credibility for your company; providing differentiation for your solutions; and getting the deal done without conceding to a price that sinks the ship.

As marketers we were really hopeful several years ago that the Internet would eclipse the need for salespeople. Everyone will buy over the net—we thought. No more salespeople—we hoped. No such luck—we found out.

Yes, the Internet dis-intermediated a lot of different human activities and streamlined many commodity transactions. But companies know that if they are to maintain a premium market position and avoid the commodity trap, or worse yet see their products sold on an Internet auction site, they need to distinguish their offerings. That requires human intervention (i.e., salespeople) to communicate differentiated value to prospects and customers.

We have to accept the fact that customer brand experience and preference are primarily established by field sales and service people. A Booz Allen & Hamilton survey[2] of the automotive industry looked at the influence on brand decision-making and loyalty generated by the Dealer (sales and service) versus the Manufacturer (product).

Their findings indicated that 85 percent of brand decision-making and brand loyalty is created at the point of sales contact and after, while only 15 percent is generated by perceptions of product value and quality. More than 50 percent of brand decision-making impact is driven by the conversations customers have with frontline sales and service people!

Sure, you can debate whether these numbers are the same for you and your industry. The 250 companies we've worked with consistently say that the number is greater than 50 percent—usually somewhere between 70 and

---

[2]Reprinted with permission from "strategy+business," the award-winning management quarterly published by Booz Allen Hamilton, www.strategy-business.com.

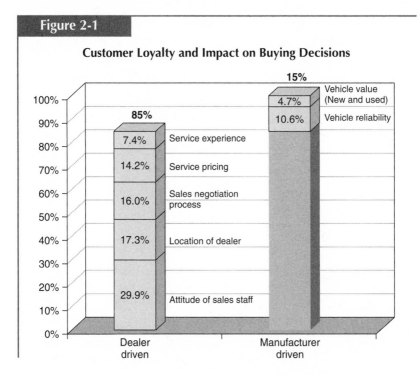

Figure 2-1

Customer Loyalty and Impact on Buying Decisions

100 percent. Regardless, the takeaway has to be that a marketer's greatest—and perhaps most overlooked—asset in creating brand equity and impact is the frontline sales and services person.

Here's a reminder: In today's near commodity or perceived parity markets, your company's last bastion of competitive differentiation is what comes out of these mouths on the front line—when the rep is sitting across a desk or conference table, 3.5 feet from your prospect or customer.

That's right. Your company's ability to craft a solution, position against the competition, and demonstrate value is at the mercy of each person in your field force. Their ability to document customer needs and successfully pull together the appropriate and most compelling best answers is what separates the winning brand from the others.

"If you don't control the last few feet of the sales process, you will lose," according to Scott M. Davis, managing director for Prophet Brand Strategy, and author of *Brand Asset Management*. "Channel member effectiveness in closing the sale is what separates great brands from others."

Sergio Zyman, author of *The End of Marketing as We Know It*, agrees: "In all categories, customers are making more brand decisions closer to the point of sale—ever heightening the value of effective communications in that area.

Your sales channel either adds or subtracts value from your brand or positioning every time they talk to a customer. They are not neutral. Every message they send is either selling or un-selling your solution."

You should be getting the picture that, increasingly, a company's success depends less on *what* they sell and more on *how* they sell it. In a highly competitive market with quickly copied features and barely discernible branding campaigns, sales rep and sales channel effectiveness become the new drivers for business success.

It's sales and services channels—not marketing—that control and drive

- brand positioning
- revenue generation
- margin protection
- customer satisfaction
- customer expansion

Unfortunately, if you ask 100 CMOs for a peek at their brand-building budgets, you will most likely see expenditures allocated completely opposite to what this study suggests. We're learning that the brand experience is primarily driven by the customer's experience with our field personnel. They can either promote or demote the brand every time their lips move. So why are we abdicating so much responsibility for that messaging to each individual sales rep, agent, broker, etc.?

If marketers are to remain relevant, we can't continue to pump big bucks into 30,000-foot corporate marketing campaigns while doing next to nothing to deliver accessible and useful sales-ready, brand-supporting messages at the all-important 3.5-foot level—the exact distance between your company's "voice to the customer" and a prospect's purchase decision.

Why CRM Came up Short

In addition to the Internet, we also thought that Customer Relationship Management (CRM) systems were the panacea to sales and marketing effectiveness. At least that's the way CRM software was sold. The idea of collecting the master customer record and all related information in one place was idealized by eager software companies as the sure path to more efficient and effective customer acquisition and retention strategies.

As a result, companies have spent millions implementing sophisticated CRM systems—because they felt they had to. CRM, however, has become a stick without a carrot. And real revenue-generating sales reps have balked.

"My challenge is to convincingly communicate the value and distinction of our offering, and then quickly provide customized follow-up information after the call. But there's nothing in our CRM system that helps me do that," according to one sales manager at a major Midwestern manufacturing firm.

Everybody knows that CRM didn't deliver on the big promise. No new news. Most enterprises have been able to wring some inefficiencies out of the customer management operations. But the focus is more on the "M" (management) than on the "R" (relationship). Companies centralize customer data, automate sales force contact and opportunity information, manage call center activities and workflow, coordinate dispatch services—all kinds of efforts aimed at getting more productivity out of front office or customer-related operations.

While it's not necessarily bad, it's just not enough. It's a no-brainer to use CRM to manage efficient relationships, keep track of data about interactions, have visibility into purchase histories, and manage your sales team's activities. The problem is that everybody is doing that. Any company can lower costs by doing some things faster. But CRM won't differentiate you, build your value message, or set you apart from the competition.

For example, most CRM systems have simply become a dictated requirement for salespeople to put their contact information in. CRM is also a place for marketing to dump their "leads." Sales reps know that increasing sales effectiveness is not about where to show up for a sales call; it's about what you say when you get there.

As a result, customer messaging, not just customer contact information, needs to be treated as one of the company's most strategic corporate assets. CRM initiatives that want to truly increase marketing and selling effectiveness need to turn their attention to what gets said before, during, and after sales cycles.

If done right, customer messaging creates empathy that earns a prospect's trust; it provides differentiation where there appears to be none; it communicates value that elevates you and your solution when all things appear equal; it protects a premium position; it helps close the deal.

Ironically, in this day when the message needs to be as clear and compelling as possible, the people creating the message—the marketing department—are miles away from the people delivering the message—the sales force.

Couple that with the fact that very few salespeople are able to translate their company's boilerplate product and marketing messaging into the prospect's business realities and align it with their professional preoccupations and corporate challenges. Now you've got a disconnect of disastrous proportions.

Why Branding Has Been a Failure: The Ongoing Struggle with Sameness

Obviously, there's a huge opportunity to be a visionary leader in marketing. But that opportunity lies downstream in being more useful throughout the customer buying process. It starts with realizing that marketing is an integrated activity with sales. It needs to be relevant throughout the entire customer development life cycle, not just the front end of customer awareness.

At the top of your organization, it's all about meeting sales objectives and revenue numbers. They aren't interested in "marketing objectives" such as brand awareness numbers or brand favorability ratings. As former Coca Cola CMO and branding czar Sergio Zyman used to say, "I don't want virtual consumption." We need real customers who can buy.

People can be aware of you, and even favorably predisposed to your brand, but if they aren't buying, then you are failing. If you are looking for a seat at the strategic table, you need a way to demonstrate your impact on increasing selling effectiveness. You need to help the company sell more stuff, more profitably.

The need to demonstrate a better return on marketing investments, particularly in the area of sales coaching, conversations, and communications support, will be job one for the savvy marketer.

Ultimately, there needs to be more process and purpose applied to managing customer messaging. What's really needed is the same rigor that world-class companies apply to such processes as supply chain management, manufacturing operations, and all the financial activities.

In his book *Escaping the Black Hole: Minimizing the Damage from the Marketing-Sales Disconnect,* author Bob Schmonsees points out that we could really use a *Marketing Bill of Materials*—a repeatable, structured approach to ensuring that the company consistently creates, delivers, and manages better marketing and sales messaging.

Most current marketing messaging and sales support discipline has never evolved past creating graphic and style guidelines to help ensure brand consistency or mandating the insertion of high-level value propositions into every communication—whether they fit or not.

Today's leading consultative sales methodologies, such as Customer-Centric Selling®, Solution Selling®, SPIN Selling®, Value Selling®, and others, are focused on helping salespeople create a brand experience based on *how* they sell, not just *what* they sell. They train salespeople to help prospects and customers understand the value of a company's solution—within the context of their business roles and goals.

Marketing's approach to building brand strategy, positioning statements, and "value propositions" has been woefully misaligned with these 3.5-foot-level sales approaches. Marketing is still too company- and product-centric. In a hypercompetitive market, this breeds an ongoing struggle with sameness, blandness, and a general lack of separation within today's big company branding campaigns and sales value propositions.

The following is a powerful illustration of the problem. A recent advertising trade magazine review of a Fortune 50 company's new branding campaign said,

> *The ads are graphically cool. They boast trendy combinations of colors and type-faces and smartly designed images. The tagline has a nice flow and urgency, but it doesn't really distinguish them from the rest of its competitors. And while the rest of the campaign is nicely integrated and intelligent, it never truly achieves that differentiation either.*

Put yourself in this scenario for a second. You are the CMO responsible for marketing at this company. You have one of the richest branding budgets in the world. You hire one of the best agencies in the world. After spending months and millions to create the campaign, and tens of millions to run it, what did you get? You got "me too."

Avoiding parity in brand positioning is a major struggle for every major company. So, if your branding campaign doesn't hold up to scrutiny at the 30,000-foot level, how will it ever translate into something actionable where your sales force can explain the difference between themselves and the competition? It won't, and they won't. You'll continue to sink deeper into something we call "No Brand's Land," which we'll discuss later in the book.

A recent poll by *BtoB Magazine* asked marketing people (not salespeople) to grade themselves on how well they prepare and provide sales support messaging and materials. Fully 70 percent gave themselves a "D" or "F." If that's the case when we grade ourselves, what grade do we think we'd get from the field?

There is tremendous pain, wasted effort, and lost opportunity associated with unusable marketing messaging and support created in the name of sales support. It's not a new phenomenon. Why does this keep happening?

For starters, too many marketers tend to pass off field marketing and sales support as "tactical" functions, preferring instead to apply themselves to

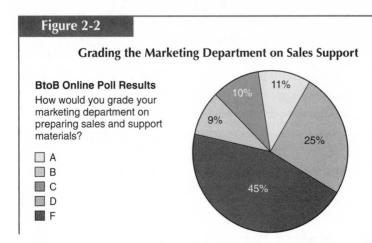

Figure 2-2

Grading the Marketing Department on Sales Support

BtoB Online Poll Results
How would you grade your marketing department on preparing sales and support materials?

☐ A
☐ B
■ C
☐ D
■ F

11%
10%
9%
25%
45%

more upstream strategic activities such as branding, value propositions, and market research, among others.

They're too busy to take the time to really understand the steps of a sales cycle and the customer buying process. They delegate the very words a salesperson is going to say to a customer down to a marketing communications specialist or agency copywriter who haven't stepped foot into the field, let alone a customer selling situation.

Ironically, many of these same marketers are completely dependent on the sales force's ability to create an opportunity for their offerings, and then carry on an intelligent conversation with a customer about how that offering meets their business needs.

We need to turn customer messaging into a strategic operation. Companies must realize that what they say to customers, and how they say it, may be their last remaining point of differentiation. We should be begging for an approach that helps everyone get on the same page for creating more customer-relevant messaging, delivering more sales-ready communications, and equipping more customer-focused conversations. In other words, move customer messaging from tribal knowledge to strategic corporate asset.

"Today's selling has less to do with the right choice of products than with the right choice of words," according to Gerhard Gschwandtner, publisher of "Selling Power Magazine." "That's why savvy managers demand that sales and marketing act as a team to create better customer message management."

"What I find most compelling about the concept of Customer Message Management is marketing's responsibility to create meaningful content that can be tied to the sales process," says Joe Galvin, VP and Research Director for Gartner Group, a leading analyst firm. "Salespeople need marketing content that is flexible and dynamic enough to meet the challenge of each selling interaction. That allows you to really make your salespeople powerful."

"We need to solve the lack of usefulness and consistency in brand and customer messaging at the all-important point of sale, as well as the lack of connection between marketing content and the revenue-generating activities of a company," according to Don Schultz, professor of integrated marketing communications at Northwestern University. "This means marketing has to overcome the lack of credibility with the sales force in providing anything that makes them more productive."

Key Chapter Take-Aways

- **Up to 90 percent** of the marketing messages and materials created for sales support is unused, or is used inappropriately.
- **Reps spend up to 60 hours** a month finding and using marketing messages to support specific sales opportunities.
- **Nearly 100 percent** of reps create or recreate your marketing materials for use with customers and prospects.
- Marketing has become a "bummer of a birthmark"; becoming **more relevant to revenue generation** is a matter of moving up in your company or moving on.

The next chapter gives a name and a structure to our practical, repeatable solution: Customer Message Management.

CHAPTER 3

THE SALES FRONTLINE: WELCOME TO NO BRAND'S LAND

After reading the previous two chapters we should all be on the same page in understanding that marketing needs to move further downstream—from 30,000 feet toward the 3.5-foot customer conversation—to be more relevant to sales success. And we should now agree that salespeople and channel partners are our most important means of accomplishing this objective.

From this point forward, we will be covering new ground and mapping uncharted territory. That's because when it comes to successfully mending the disconnect and integrating marketing with sales, much has been whined about, but little has been done.

Marketing academics and practitioners have long preached the merits of integrated marketing communications (IMC). Books have been written, classes taught, and even entire college departments are dedicated to the subject. The idea is simple: Develop a clear brand positioning concept and then ensure that all customer communications and touch-points, whether via mass advertising, direct mail, the web, or another medium, work together to support the brand.

Ironically, this practice has tended to neglect the direct salesperson or channel partner as part of the "integration" plan. We recently received an email from someone who had read one of our articles on Customer Message Management and the link between marketing and sales in an online newsletter. She said that she was reviewing a new textbook on IMC, and stated, incredulously, that nowhere in the book did it discuss how to connect the IMC strategy with the field sales process. And that she was personally going to interject a new chapter on the subject.

Strike another blow for marketing relevance. But the fact that this textbook had made it that far without an ode to sales integration speaks to the challenges ahead.

To help us better deal with the challenge, we had to name it. If you can't measure what you can't count, then you can't fix a problem if you can't name it and clearly describe it.

We call the problem *No Brand's Land*®. It's that black hole where all good marketing intentions created at the 30,000-foot headquarters level seem to

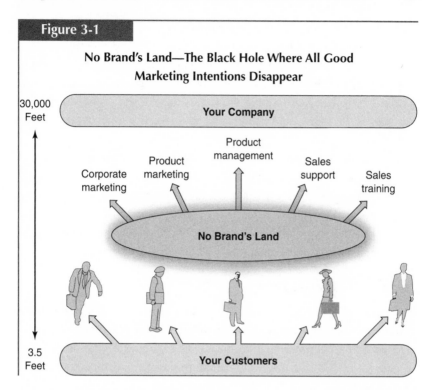

Figure 3-1

No Brand's Land—The Black Hole Where All Good
Marketing Intentions Disappear

30,000 Feet

Your Company

Corporate marketing

Product marketing

Product management

Sales support

Sales training

No Brand's Land

3.5 Feet

Your Customers

disappear before reaching the all-important 3.5-foot level—never to be heard from again.

On one side of No Brand's Land, brand marketers can control all of the execution: The advertising campaign coordinates with the media coverage generated by your PR firm, which integrates nicely with the trade show booth and your Web site. We even put corporate design guidelines in place to make sure all collaterals and presentations headed to the field are consistent in look and feel.

On the other side of No Brand's Land, your salespeople are still doing their own thing. They waste time looking for and/or creating their own ad hoc sales materials that they feel they are missing. They are cutting and pasting from old proposals with outdated information and incorrect messages. They're fabricating home-grown, "clandestine" collateral tools and *Microsoft PowerPoint* presentations that are, at best, inconsistent with your corporate positioning, and at worst, downright wrong.

Most frightening for marketers is that these cobbled-together documents have to walk the halls of your prospective customers, representing your company's brand and pitching your products at the most critical points in the sales process. Ouch.

Adding insult to injury, the field-fabrication virus tends to spread exponentially, perpetuating bad information—ineffective and inconsistent sales messaging and dialogues—across the channel on their intranet, *Lotus Notes,* or some other forum for exchanging tribal knowledge. In one recent workshop, a sales participant proudly showed us that he had installed Publisher software on his laptop and had created an entire portfolio of "clandestine collateral."

As a result, even if marketers accept the need to move their strategies further "downstream"—into the hands and mouths of sales reps and various channel partners—they are still puzzled by exactly how to adapt their 30,000-foot brand strategy or their stovepiped product marketing organizations to the needs of individual sales representatives delivering personalized positioning, presentations, and proposals at the 3.5-foot level.

Escaping No Brand's Land

The only way to escape this No Brands Land is to link marketing content creation and sales content delivery together to create a common approach to facilitating the customer buying process. The companies that do this best also are going to be the first to separate from the market sameness described in Chapter 2.

"For marketing to be meaningful and contribute to revenue-generating activities, it must provide messaging that aligns with a company's sales process, which is hopefully built around how the customer wants to buy," says Joe Galvin, a vice president of the Gartner Consulting Group, specializing in sales effectiveness.

Companies need to begin applying strategic corporate discipline around Customer Message Management. There must be more rigor, structure, and emphasis on the practice. At the highest levels, executives must ask themselves these questions:

Is my messaging customer-relevant? That is, does it represent the conversations you want to take place with customers? Have you aligned messaging in response to customer goals, requirements, and business needs—instead of product feature function—and provided corresponding supporting evidence? Is it formatted in a way that is useful to customers?

Is my content sales-ready? In other words, does it conform to the way you want your salespeople to sell? Is it organized so they can easily find the right content at the right time based on the needs of the customers and sales force? Can it be composed into a format that is deliverable—easily and consistently across each rep in every channel, in accordance with your best practices, training, and sales process?

This may not sound like rocket science. But what seems logical in principle doesn't always get done in practice. Think about your own corporate positioning, value propositions, product marketing, sales training, coaching, and collaterals. Are they built in the way customers like to be communicated with? Are they delivered the way salespeople can best access and use them in a typical sales cycle?

Increasing your sales channels' effectiveness will be the number-one strategic objective for improving top- and bottom-line corporate performance in the coming years. As a result, equipping more effective customer messaging—and in turn, the resultant selling conversations and collaterals—could be the most important marketing strategy you employ right now.

Before you relegate this idea to a simple marketing communications tactic or training program, think about this possibility: In an era of information overload, product sameness, and brand blurring, what's going to set you apart? What's going to ensure your brand strategy is successful? More and more, this battle will be fought in the trenches, not in Superbowl ads.

According to the book *Simplicity: The New Competitive Advantage in a World of More, Better, Faster*,[1] "the most conservative estimates show business information doubling every three years." Bottom line: At least every 1,100 days your prospects' and customers' ability to transform information into decisions and productive work becomes twice as important. Because in that time, the amount of information they will need to ignore, organize, translate, communicate, and build into solutions will double.

In today's overloaded, complicated environment, your company's ability to help order, make sense of, and connect all of this information into something meaningful to your prospects and customers will distinguish you among all of the other "noise makers." You will literally compete on the clarity of your customer messaging.

Tomorrow's successful brand strategy will be executed through the field—by the individual men and women of your sales and services teams. As a result, you're going to have to move your brand-building efforts further downstream. You're going to have to get a little messy. You will have to mix it up with sales reps, services reps, and even customers.

---

[1] Bill Jensen, *Simplicity: The New Competitive Advantage in a World of More, Better, Faster*. New York: Perseus Books, 2001.

The Value Proposition Myth

One key for getting through No Brand's Land is for companies to get much closer to the 3.5-foot-level customer conversation—not the fake ones they have in focus groups, but real ones that happen in the decision-making process. And in this process you'll realize that differentiation can no longer be obtained by *communicating the value of your company*, or its products and services. Rather, you must learn how to *create value for the customer,* as you seek to understand how you will meet *their* needs, solve *their* problems, or help them achieve *their* goals.

The real challenge is that too many product marketers, and ultimately sales and services people, really understand their products but not enough about their customers' "problems." Product pitches and sales arguments are focused on individual product features, benefits, and price points.

As a result, most products in most markets begin to look and sound so much alike that there is no perceived differentiation, and companies begin finding themselves losing competitions they think they should win or discounting so severely that even if they win the deal they aren't sure they actually won anything.

A good way to understand this concept is to take a step back and see the presumptuous nature of the value proposition: We are going to propose or worse yet, tell, the client what a solution is, and what they should value about our offering. This is pure folly. In a sales conversation, only the customer can tell you when something is a solution, and when they think it will provide value. Determining value is the exclusive domain of the customer decision-maker. Or you could say value is in the eye of the beholder (or buyer in this case). Once the prospect understands and can explain back to you how you can help them achieve their desired outcomes, then, and only then, have you created a solution and offered anything of value.

As a result, marketing departments and sales forces that continue to communicate a brand position from the company out, and propose the value of their products, are doomed to fall into the vast wasteland of perceived parity and commodity considerations where all the leading companies appear to have the same thing to offer—and all that's left to argue is price.

Instead, we must challenge ourselves to *create customer value* to survive. We can do this by following a very simple formula that links our capabilities to specific business needs and client profiles. It's at this intersection where we can finally begin to create customer-focused value messaging—what we call "value creation."

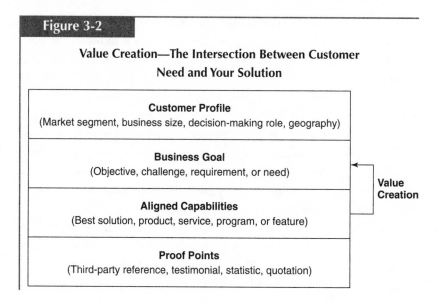

Figure 3-2

Value Creation—The Intersection Between Customer
Need and Your Solution

Customer Profile
(Market segment, business size, decision-making role, geography)

Business Goal
(Objective, challenge, requirement, or need)

Value
Creation

Aligned Capabilities
(Best solution, product, service, program, or feature)

Proof Points
(Third-party reference, testimonial, statistic, quotation)

Some may be tempted to dismiss this as a remedial marketing concept. We challenge you to review your most recent brand-positioning statements, collateral, direct marketing, advertising, product training, and sales messaging. How often do your value propositions reflect this all-important intersection? Or are they more generic, static, and product-centric in nature? Also, are your salespeople using all your materials—or are they saying, "We can't use this stuff, we sound too arrogant . . . or we need to talk about the customer!"

Our intentions as marketers are honorable, but our actions are often still trapped in the inertia of company- and product-centric marketing. We don't fully understand or appreciate the nuances of the customer decision-making process and the requirement for intelligent sales conversation that align our story with the customer's problems, goals, or needs.

As a result, our marketing and sales messaging does not conform to the way consultative salespeople need to sell—nor does it reflect the conversations they are having with customers.

Just-in-Time, Opportunity-Specific Learners

Another key to crossing over No Brand's Land is to deliver messaging and content in a way that works the way salespeople work. By their nature, salespeople are "just-in-time, opportunity-specific" learners. They learn something when they actually need to use it. In the field, this comes to light when a salesperson encounters a particular customer type with a specific business issue. What that salesperson really wants is to be able to push a button and find out *right then* what the company's best answer is for *that opportunity.*

That's today's customer messaging reality. It's no longer about general product expertise. It's about customer conversation competency—having the ability to be fluent based on the customer opportunity. Unfortunately, our traditional messaging methodologies, content, and delivery media are built completely opposite. They are constructed around products, not customer opportunities, and they are presented as either classroom cramming or generic, static information as opposed to situational scenarios or conversations.

Something has to give. If we've learned anything over the years, it's that trying to change salespeople to match our preferred messaging and collateral approaches doesn't work. It's like wrangling our children for dinner. We struggle getting them to the table—and then we can't get them to sit still long enough to eat once they get there.

Unlike children, from whom we can demand first-time obedience and bring consequences for inappropriate actions, we have no such authority over salespeople. So we are left to either wring our hands and complain about these "coin-operated, ADD disasters," or figure out a way to align our content creation and delivery process to the way they prefer to access and use it.

Back to our just-in-time, opportunity-specific learning concept:

Just-in-time. We must make the right information available precisely when and where salespeople need it.

We've made some progress in this area. A whole category has sprung up over the past decade to deal with this challenge. But electronic marketing information, intranets, and other technology-driven systems still miss the mark. Despite providing the field with easier, online, 24/7 access to content, we're still not seeing significant improvements in ramp-up and customer conversation competency.

That's because automating the content delivery process simply improves operational efficiency, not effectiveness. As the saying goes, if the process and content stinks, technology will only increase and speed up the stench.

JIT marketing content delivery strategies miss the second, and probably most important, half of the sales learning equation—it's not "opportunity-specific."

Opportunity-specific. We must create content in a way that salespeople can intuitively access and dynamically assemble just the information they need for the customer conversation they find themselves in.

Today's messaging is still too product centric versus customer focused, and it's not applicable as part of the salesperson's actual activities in a sales cycle. Whether it's preparing for a customer conversation, developing a sales presentation, or producing follow-up letters and proposal documentation, there are specific moments of truth in consultative sales cycles where a salesperson wants and needs the right support.

Customer messaging needs to be available, and occur, in real-time, during real-world sales opportunities. This requires a critical alignment between marketing, training, and sales process to create a new marketing sales support model. One that's based on the critical interactions you expect your salespeople to have in the consultative sales cycle.

The process of engaging a customer in a consultative conversation and solutions sales cycle has been well documented. Sales methodology companies have codified the process into key steps and developed training classes to help B and C sales reps do what A reps do intuitively, which is to build solutions and create value for customers—versus communicate product features and benefits.

These sales methodology trainers each claim to have their own intellectual property, and they push their preferred selling approaches, but they ultimately come up short in the same area: "They build the engine, but don't fill the tank with fuel."

What does that mean? It means they teach a salesperson how to conduct a more consultative sales cycle, give them the milestones, templates, and reminders, but don't provide the actual content that will make the process "go." The sales rep knows *who* to speak with, and the *type* of conversation they should have, but they don't have the words to say when they get there.

So where are you going to get this fuel—that is, content—for the sales process engine? Will it come from product marketing and training? Click . . . click . . . click. Engine's still not turning over. That's because your newly-minted consultative sales process is at odds with the company's product training program.

Even though your salespeople have been trained to "diagnose" customer needs before they "prescribe" product answers, your product training continues to promote individual product features, functions, and benefits. The conflict is exacerbated by marketing and communications tools that also are primarily product centric, silo'd, and have no connection to the realities of a consultative sales cycle.

As a result, at the core of Customer Message Management is an opportunity-specific content creation and delivery strategy. There are two key components to this strategy:

- First, the content must be created in the context of the most typical customer profiles, their business needs, and most appropriate answers.

- Second, the content must be made available as part of the actual preparations, conversations, presentations, and documentation that occur in a sales cycle.

The premise is simple: Align your messaging to customer needs; make your best customer messaging easily available to every rep and for every call; and enable quick, personalized follow-up based on the needs of each opportunity.

The promise is even greater: Decrease rep ramp-up time, reduce non-selling time, improve B and C player performance, create consistency across sales channels, along with providing assurances that marketing investments are having a tangible impact on revenue-generating activities.

Key Chapter Take-Aways

- **No Brand's Land** is the black hole where all good marketing intentions created at the 30,000-foot headquarters level disappear before reaching the all-important 3.5-foot level—never to be heard from again.
- Like it or not, **your salespeople are doing their own thing**—creating ad hoc sales materials, cutting and pasting from old proposals with outdated information and incorrect messages, and fabricating collateral and presentations that are, at best, inconsistent with your corporate positioning, or at worst, downright wrong.
- The real challenge is that we understand our products, but not enough about customers' problems. As a result, we "propose value" based on product features—instead of "**creating value**" by linking our best capabilities to their real business problems.
- Salespeople are **opportunity-specific, just-in-time learners.** If messaging and training are not in the context of the sales process, then sales will not see the content—or the marketers who created it—as relevant to the way they sell solutions.
- The **premise of CMM** is simple: Align your messaging to customer needs; make your best customer messaging easily available to every rep and for every call; and enable quick, personalized follow-up based on the needs of each opportunity.

The next chapter describes the process for creating customer messaging—and the resources or people who can make it happen for your company.

CHAPTER 4

PRINCIPLES OF CUSTOMER MESSAGE MANAGEMENT

If someone wants to begin performing Customer Message Management today, what are the absolute first things they have to do? This question was posed to a group of elite presenters and panelists brought together by the American Marketing Association during its CMM Forum Series, which held its inaugural session in June 2002 at the *University of Chicago Gleacher Center* in Chicago. Here are the four guiding principles that emerged:

Figure 4-1

Principles of Customer Message Management

CMM Principle #1	CMM Principle #2	CMM Principle #3	CMM Principle #4
Integrate marketing and sales processes	Create customer-relevant messaging	Sales cycle-relevant collaterals	Centralized, online accessibility
Provides common approach and language for creating and delivering content and support that helps facilitate the customer buying process	Puts messaging in customer context based on who they are, and what they are trying to achieve	Customer messaging is relevant and useful across the sales cycle in critical moments of truth and for advancing a deal toward close	A single, centralized, online repository of your best selling messages makes it easier for marketing to manage and sales to use

1. Integrate Marketing and Sales Processes

Functional silos need to be replaced with shared objectives. Unstructured activities need to be structured and aligned in an integrated, cross-functional approach to acquiring, keeping, and expanding customers.

The issue is both organizational and attitudinal. Maybe it requires that marketing and sales have to exist under one executive who can put their foot down and say, "You guys need to play together." At least we must create enough common sense of purpose and process that ensures both sides are pushing and pulling in the same direction!

2. Create Customer-Relevant Messaging

Messaging needs to be more relevant to prospects and customers based on their context—who they are and what they are trying to achieve. Customers want to buy; they don't like being sold.

Specifically, customers want to buy from someone who can most clearly demonstrate how a company's capabilities align to help them solve a problem, meet a need, or achieve a goal. This means we must move beyond individual product feature and function-based messaging to more customer-relevant messaging.

3. Deliver More Sales-Cycle-Relevant Collaterals

Marketing and sales communications tools traditionally have been driven more by corporate design guidelines and standards, as well as award-winning designers, than by the practicalities and realities of the customer interaction.

Packaging and delivering messaging into formats and outputs that support the specific steps of a best practice solutions or consultative sales cycle increases the utility of the content and the potential impact marketing can have deeper into the process. It also gives marketers more consistency and control over message delivery that is currently out of control.

4. Provide Centralized, Online Accessibility

Better messaging, delivered in more useful tools, still needs to be easily accessible in ways that work for remote, distributed sales forces and channel partners. Making sure busy reps, working on their own, can quickly get to the most appropriate messaging and materials is critical to closing the loop on an improved Customer Message Management process.

What's required is a single, online repository for all marketing and sales support. Most importantly, it must provide a variety of paths for intuitively accessing the needed content to support sales conversations, presentations, and documentation. In addition, it must provide the ability to coach and reinforce the preferred consultative selling process, while integrating all activities with the company's customer relationship management database.

It's the *Tough* Stuff, not the *Fluff* Stuff

Driving consistent and compelling messages from the company through the various selling touch-points and channels is what separates the great brands from the also-rans. Many companies invest millions in their brand strategy and messaging platform, but they struggle to transform it into the everyday language and dialogues that drive sales cycles.

Customer Message Management was developed to help create more customer-relevant, sales-ready conversations—whether they occur as self-service Web site experiences, or are part of sales cycle presentations and documentation.

CMM is practical, not theory. For the first time, you can get specific direction, examples, tools, and templates to push the 30,000-foot "brand promise" to the all-important 3.5-foot "brand experience" level—the exact distance between your selling voice and the key customer decision-maker.

It's Not *What* You Sell, but *How* You Sell That Counts

In today's increasingly complex and competitive marketing and sales environment, it's nearly impossible to differentiate on features and benefits. Nearly every advantage is copied or eclipsed in months. Customers know this. They assume that the top two or three competitors in any given market have approximately the same offerings. That's why they believe they can throw you into a "competitive bake-off" to see who will blink first and most when it comes to discounting and pricing concessions.

Since the basic market assumption is that everyone is the same when it comes to the *what* you sell (product capabilities), *how* you sell (message creation and delivery) becomes much more important. We could argue that your customer messages—the words that you use to create a vision match and buying commitment with customers, along with your ability to consistently communicate them to and through the field—are your most strategic asset, if not your last bastion of competitive differentiation.

That's why the Customer Message Management approach presented in this book is helping train companies to translate and transform brand platforms and product positioning into the kind of messaging that powers successful sales coaching, training, and ultimately, customer presentations, documentation, and conversations.

Product Marketing Silos Are Holding Us Back

Since product marketers often P&L responsibility, they charge myopically and parochially into creating the ultimate product training, sales information, marketing content, and customer communications toolkits—all extolling the exceptional virtues of their offering.

Essentially, they equip salespeople to tell the customer, "Here's what it is. Here's what it does. Here's why it's good for you. And here are some ways we think we're better than the competition." Is that a familiar outline for product launches and sales kits at your company?

If a product manager or marketer is ever going to help a salesperson create and sell a "solution" for a customer—whether in a conversation, presentation, or documentation—they will have to show how that product, or particular features of that product, can be applied to help the customer accomplish something they desire.

Unfortunately, too many of us have a good grasp of our products, but we don't know enough about our customers' goals and business problems. As a result, aligning products and capabilities with real-world customer needs is left to chance with only the most intuitive, consultative "A" sales reps doing it naturally.

We have an opportunity to "codify" the intuitive solution selling approach and pre-build marketing messages and sales content that clone the customer conversations, presentations, and documentations of your "A" salespeople.

This requires a transformation of your sales coaching and customer-facing communications. Here's one way to think about it: We need to move from traditional company product-centric messaging to customer problem- (or goal)-centric messaging.

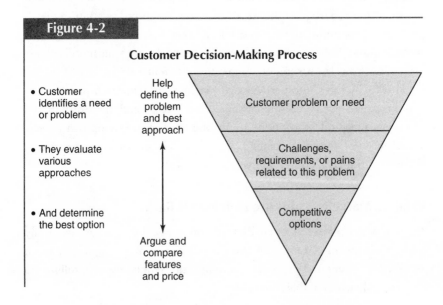

Figure 4-2

Customer Decision-Making Process

- Customer identifies a need or problem

- They evaluate various approaches

- And determine the best option

Help define the problem and best approach

Argue and compare features and price

Customer problem or need

Challenges, requirements, or pains related to this problem

Competitive options

Aligning to the Customer Decision-Making Process

The first task in Customer Message Management is defining how your prospects or customers make decisions. Roughly, most customers work through three phases:

- First, they identify a strategic business problem that they need to solve, or they establish an important goal they want to achieve.
- Next, they examine the various ways that they can solve that problem or achieve that goal. They ask themselves, what pain points, challenges, or obstacles prevent us from solving the problem or achieving the goal? Then they prioritize the areas that they need to invest in, and they weigh the alternatives for dealing with the issue.
- Finally, they choose a product or service category that they believe will solve the problem, and they seek out competitive vendors to pitch the opportunity.

Once a customer reaches phase three in this thought process, they've already established a detailed set of evaluation criteria around a particular product or service, and their decision has narrowed to a specific feature set and price.

Inevitably, the stovepiped product organizations described earlier will create messages, selling strategies, and tools for the last phase—when the customer has created what amounts to a *competitive "bake-off."* The evidence is sitting in our marketing portals—product-focused content and communications, competitive comparisons, unique selling propositions, and objection handlers.

By positioning our products for the bake-off, we've abdicated the other critical decisions completely to the customer and their committees. We've elected to wait for the RFP, or for a "qualified prospect"—one who has already defined the answer to their problem. As a result, we miss the real opportunity for solution selling and differentiated positioning that comes from selling at the "customer problem" level versus the traditional "company product" approach.

When you shift from traditional company product marketing to customer problem (goal)-oriented marketing, your job as a marketer changes. Marketing needs to build messaging and tools that equip salespeople to help customers define the problem and shape the best answer—in the customer's context.

This requires you to more proactively identify the key players in a decision, determine their most pressing business needs, and map your capabilities to those issues. Then you can create value in the context of the customer's problem—rather than generically proposing the benefit of a feature.

Given this structure, you can then codify the conversations, presentations, and documentation that enable customers to buy your solutions. Help your sales channels consult and guide a customer through needs discovery and solution development—versus just reactively responding to customer requirements.

Example: How the Customer Problem (Goal) Approach Changes Everything

Take a minute now to think about how your business unit or your company describes its product or services. Chances are that the main thrust of the messages and so-called value propositions are really just features and benefits of the product. Too often we are guilty of telling all about what "it" can do, and how "it" can do that better than the competition.

Customers are savvy. They know that no product or service can do something by itself. What they care about is how they, or their staff, use or apply your product or service to help them solve the problem or achieve the goal. Your challenge is to help customers envision themselves using your solution in the context of their business situation.

Example of Traditional Company Product-Centric Approach

In the "company product" approach, you might say something like this: "Here's our new ABC 600 multifunction, wide-format copier printing system. *Its* new Posi-Derflex Torque Control provides smoother motor operation, so *it* minimizes paper jams and disruptions, enabling you to avoid costly downtime and unwanted waste."

You should quickly see that this content, which previously may have looked like an excellent feature/benefit statement, is hopelessly mired in the last step of the customer decision-making process we described earlier—the competitive bake-off.

In this conversation, we've probably handed the customer a data sheet on the ABC 600 and Posi-Derflex technology as we make this pronouncement. Now we've given them all the ammunition they need to send that information to two other competitors and get aggressive price quotes on similarly featured products.

Example of Proposed Customer Problem (Goal)-Centric Approach

The "customer problem" approach begins with the decision-making process that may have led to the competitive bake-off:

1. **Customer determines potential business problem/goal.** Key executives at an engineering firm are struggling with the tender/bid management process. They can't respond fast enough to invitations to tender, and the process costs too much money. They commit themselves to fixing this problem so they can win more business and be more profitable.

2. **Customer reviews pain points/alternatives.** They determine that their document management and control process, along with copying logistics, are a huge bottleneck that slows down the tenders. Is this a people training issue? Is it a matter of having more bodies? Is it a workflow or process issue? Is there something we can automate? Do we have up-to-date technologies?

3. **Customer identifies competitive options.** The company decides that its copier/printers are woefully out of date and in constant need of service. They need a new multifunction, wide-format copier printer system. Call in competitors A, B, and C.

Imagine what could happen if we created content and selling aids that coached salespeople to conduct a discussion around the customer's need to: *improve copying logistics and document management in the tender management process.*

First, we would demonstrate an understanding of the customer's business and their problems. Second, we would engage in a business discussion that helped the customer think through the problem and its impact. Third, we would help sales enable the customer buying process instead of pushing product—and pushing our sales process on the customer.

Once we refocus the conversation on this business need, we can begin to align key capabilities that our company brings to the table:

Customer XYZ needs to *improve copying logistics and document management in the tender management process. Here's how we can help* (our top three corresponding capabilities may include):

1. **Workflow consulting.** Our company provides expert consulting services that can assess your tender management process and provide best-practice recommendations for improving workflow.

2. **Distributed management software.** Our company provides the ability to manage the activities and capacities of all your printers and copiers to automatically route and reroute work to the best available tool in order to maximize capacity usage and eliminate this manual task during tender management crunch time.

3. **Posi-Derflex Torque Control.** Our company's wide-format, multi-function copier printer is the first and only to feature this functionality, which ensures maximum speed and system uptime especially at peak use times like tenders.

What's the big difference here between the company product method of pitching our ABC 600 system with Posi-Derflex Torque Control and the customer problem approach?

We've knitted together a range of capabilities (hardware, software, and services) to create a recommended solution to a higher level business problem. Now our "box" has a bigger purpose, and our new feature contributes to a greater cause. Ultimately our company can be seen as bringing together a real solution in answer to a real business problem.

This is a chance to create and sell value in the context of what the customer needs to accomplish. The customer isn't in the business of buying copier/printers and distinguishing between feature semantics and subtleties— the role we put them in with a company product approach. The customer is in the business of making a profit, which is where the customer problem marketing approach can take your messaging and sales content.

Proactively Prescribing and Populating Best Answers to Customer Problems

Here's a key point to ponder: Do you think the problem used in this example exists exclusively at one engineering firm? Or could the problem be ubiquitous across engineering firms?

Most likely, this issue is a thorn in the side of nearly all engineering firms. Why stop at engineering? It might also be a pressing issue for architecture firms, construction firms, and defense contractors where managing tenders is a big part of every day. If we build our messaging on the customer need, it opens all kinds of market potential for helping similarly distressed customers visualize themselves solving an important business problem.

Why wait until customers put out the cattle call for your product? If you know the repeatable, pressing challenges of decision-makers in your target markets, why not proactively prescribe the content that will help "load the lips" of salespeople and consistently populate the messages to support consultative sales cycles?

Today, we leave this process to chance. Or more accurately, we leave it to the top 10 percent of the salespeople who conduct these discussions intuitively. Since they will hit quota regardless, what are we doing to help the other 90 percent of the rep population that can really help us beat our number?

Your "key customer conversations" are repeatable and predictable. So you can pre-build your stories to equip intelligent, confident customer dialogue. And you can encourage sales conversations with the right levels of buyers; or in potential markets; or to stimulate find, keep, and close opportunities.

To do this, you'll need a map.

CMM Message Map™: A Messaging Model to Help You

CMM is a practical process for examining your target markets, identifying repeatable business needs, and mapping your products and services to those needs. It helps you create value for customers by building a buying vision based on a business need—while the competitor sells a box.

The first step is to build a Message Map. The Message Map starts by answering the five basic questions that consultative solution salespeople ask themselves:

1. Who am I meeting with today?
2. What are their problems, needs, and goals?
3. What can I offer that aligns with their business issues?
4. How will they use that solution to achieve "contextual" value?
5. How can I prove and differentiate these claims?

This isn't rocket science. If we can codify this process for salespeople, and it's the preferred way for customers to engage us in a consultative discussion, then we should align the marketing content creation and delivery process accordingly. *While it's not rocket science, why haven't we done it consistently as an organization?*

Probably because we don't have a committed company process—across product silos and business units—to document and institutionalize the needs of the key decision-makers in our target markets. And then use that as the platform for aligning how we can meet those needs and create value across product silos and business units. That's why we need a Message Map to bring structure and rigor to a silo'd, unstructured activity.

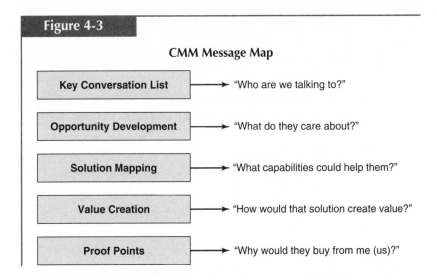

Figure 4-3

CMM Message Map

Key Conversation List	⟶ "Who are we talking to?"
Opportunity Development	⟶ "What do they care about?"
Solution Mapping	⟶ "What capabilities could help them?"
Value Creation	⟶ "How would that solution create value?"
Proof Points	⟶ "Why would they buy from me (us)?"

Let's look at this process to understand the structure and strategy. In Section 2 we'll walk through each step with examples and templates.

Step One: Key Conversation List   *Segmentation and Prioritization*

At their most basic, selling and marketing are a series of conversations. Whether it's a self-service Web site hit, a trade show visit, a direct mail response, a contact center interaction, a direct sales presentation or rep or dealer calls—the "customer conversation" is where all of your hard work on branding, positioning, product features, and benefits will either resonate or not.

In this step your team will segment your market, prioritize where your company needs to make revenue impact, and define the key decision-makers that make or break your deals in these key segments. We call this a *key conversation list*.

Step Two: Opportunity Development   *Identify Business Needs and Challenges*

The next step is gaining a real-world understanding of why decision-makers buy. Why would they open your mailing, visit your Web site, read your advertising, or entertain your salesperson for 30 minutes? What business goals are they trying to achieve? What are the greatest problems or challenges hindering their success? What pressing business needs lead them to evaluate vendors?

In this step you'll determine—in the customer's words and from the customer's perspective—the business problems and goals of each decision-maker on your key conversation list. We call this *opportunity development*.

Step Three: Solution Mapping   *Align Capabilities to Business Needs*

In the eye of the customer (the only person who can say whether or not it's a solution), your ability to create a solution is based on your ability to map the capabilities of your product, service, or technology to the buyers' goals, problems, or needs. The only verbiage needed is a clear, concise description of how your capabilities can be applied or used by the customer to address the business need.

In this step your team will CMM-align your company's capabilities to each business problem or goal for decision-maker on the key conversation list, and then create important, usually neglected messages called "diagnostic questions" and "usage scenarios." We call this *solution mapping*.

Step Four: Value Creation   *Create Relevant, Meaningful Value Statements*

Too many marketing people "communicate benefits" when the customer really wants a link between your solution and their needs—value creation versus value proposition. Value creation occurs when you demonstrate the relevant impact they can achieve when your product helps them solve a problem, achieve a goal, or meet a need.

Your team will pinpoint the unique intersection between the customer profile, their specific business need, and the "mapped" solution. It's at this intersection where we can write a true value statement. Without the customer context, marketers are creating generic feature/benefit statements based on what *they* think the product does, and why *they* think it is good for the customer. We call this *value creation*.

Step Five: Proof Point Plotting   *Validate Your Solution's Value*

No value story is complete without a reference, testimony, or some sort of third-party proof point to support your claims and convince customers of your competence. However, finding the right proof points at the right time often proves difficult.

You team will follow the process to identify the best-fitting testimonial, customer quotations, statistics, study results, or other form of outside validation related to meeting the corresponding business need for the targeted decision-maker. This exercise is called *proof point plotting*.

Sales-Ready Conversations, Presentations, and Documentation

Using the five-step process to identify and develop messages is one thing. Using the messages consistently across customer touch-points is another— and it's critical. The key to successfully implementing CMM is delivering your new customer messages in a form and format that supports the customer decision-making process.

Throughout the customer buying process, you can identify "moments of truth"—important interactions and conversations that start with awareness and continue through purchase and implementation. Understanding the objective of each interaction, the required messages, and the best structure or medium for that content is a discipline that every marketing and communications person needs to learn. We call this *sales cycle-relevant marketing*.

In many companies today, you can find too many individual product marketing managers—sometimes even sitting in adjoining cubicles—with separate agendas and incentives. Each one creates, delivers, and manages contradictory portfolios of customer communications and sales support tools. Think about how your company compares to the following not so uncommon scenario.

Product Marketer #1—The Mother of All PowerPoints   This product marketer decides she wants to send out 100-slide *PowerPoint* decks to the field to help explain the product. She wants to give salespeople the flexibility to mix and match any of these slides to showcase myriad, dazzling product features.

Product Marketer #2—The "Foldure" Guy   This product marketer wants to provide some detailed support and flexibility to sales reps, so he creates a combination folder and brochure he calls the "foldure." The foldure contains some static brochure pages with a pocket in the back that can hold a combination of 30 different flyers and cut sheets describing the product and its features.

Product Marketer #3—The Coffee Cup and Confetti Clown   This poor product marketer struggles to get mindshare in the field. She might have an exciting product, but can't seem to crack the sales psyche and get included on deals. So she sends out a dimensional sales support package that includes a coffee cup with the product name on it. The cup is filled with confetti that flies out and into the salesperson's lap after opening the mailer, and the product features are oh-so-cleverly silk-screened onto individual instant coffee packets.

Now imagine the company's sales reps returning from a consultative-selling sales call after uncovering business needs. The rep thinks that the solution will cross all three of these product areas. How is the rep supposed to assemble a meaningful customer response with this kind of support? In a timely fashion? With any consistency or quality?

Not only are we asking the rep to be a writer and graphic artist; we're asking them to fabricate our company's best-answer solution and core messaging.

Because our messages tend to be product silo'd, most collateral and other tools are never used in the sales cycle. The AMA estimated that upwards of 90 percent of what gets created in the name of sales support doesn't get used as intended, if at all. At best, we find they are used early in the cycle to create interest and demonstrate viability. Or they are used as stuffing at the back of a proposal or presentation package—for "thud factor."

During the heavy lifting in a sales cycle, there's a very different set of documents that emerge (and get created on hard drives throughout sales) to support the formal or ad hoc sales process.

These documents are usually the ones that end up driving customer conversations and ultimately walking the customer's hallways representing your company's best and final selling messages.

The biggest threats posed by clandestine collateral include

1. **Lack of brand consistency.** How do you give marketing and sales "one voice" and present one voice to the customer when the "collateralization" of these all-important sales conversations and follow-up are left to chance and the whims of individual sales reps.

2. **Too many inaccuracies.** Who knows what bad data and bad branding gets perpetuated when the field is left on its own to fabricate its customer collateral—in the name of your company.

3. **Costly inefficiencies.** Corrupted selling time or non-selling time is only made worse when reps have to use valuable time preparing custom responses, presentations, and proposals.

4. **Reduced effectiveness.** Not every salesperson is a great writer, or even has enough knowledge of the best answers and/or approaches to create the most compelling or persuasive messages.

Mapping to "Moments Of Truth"

The absolute key to this concept is designing and delivering messaging content in a form and format that supports important milestones throughout the sales cycle. To figure this out, you must work with key reps, channel partners, and sales management to determine the steps in your company's sanctioned or ad hoc sales process, and identify the key conversations and collaterals required at each "moment of truth."

Figure 4-4

Sales-Ready Document Design Workshop

Call Preparation	Problem Definition	Solution Development	Value Proposition	Detailed Proposal

- Identify the steps of the sales cycle

- Understand the objectives of each moment of truth

- Identify the messaging requirements

- Determine the content type required for support

- Develop delivery and access approach

This requires your team to conduct a sales collateral audit and a *Sales Cycle-Relevant Document Design Workshop*. Such a workshop can't be conducted in a vacuum. Just as in the messaging process, it is critical that you involve successful salespeople in this step.

An audit of your current collateral collection will determine who, what, when, why, and how messages are delivered to customers. It will help you prioritize or reallocate where your marketing dollars are spent in support of sales.

Institutionalizing this approach may require you to implement one of several emerging technology solutions that enable salespeople to automatically compose personal, relevant communications tools—based on specific customer business requirements—for each unique sales opportunity.

Marketing's big win is that every salesperson—even within a multichannel environment—will more likely communicate a consistent message. Sales will be thrilled to have content, coaching, and collaterals that work the way they want to work.

Imagine the brand-building power unleashed when your sales channels deliver an integrated, powerful, and pre-approved message at every moment of truth!

It can be done.

Key Chapter Take-Aways

- **CMM is practical, not theory.** It pushes the 30,000-foot "brand promise" to the all-important 3.5-foot "brand experience" level—the exact distance between your selling voice and the key customer decision-maker.

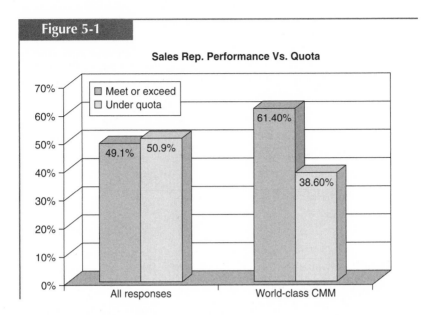

Figure 5-1

Sales Rep. Performance Vs. Quota

Where Dismal Gets Dangerous

The study next analyzed sales performance in terms of forecasting accuracy and outcome. For the ten years CSO Insights has been conducting this survey, forecasting accuracy has consistently been a challenge for sales and marketing executives.

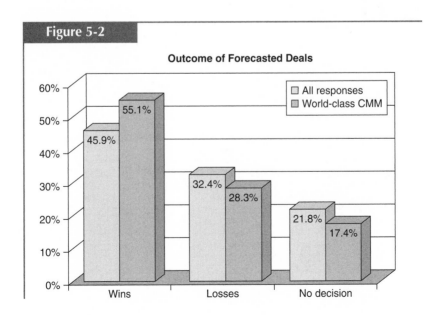

Figure 5-2

Outcome of Forecasted Deals

This is bad news. Beyond hurting the credibility of the sales force and the person in charge of it, this level of volatility—or lack of predictability—minimizes the effectiveness of several other functional areas within a company. If target revenue numbers are greatly exceeded but not forecast, opportunities to leverage this growth with added staffing or new programs ahead of the competition might be lost. Alternatively, forecasting deals that are delayed—or, worse, do not come in at all—can result in companies overspending and/or overstaffing when they should be paring back.

Contrast this with the performance of the study group. The World-Class CMM organizations registered almost 20 percent (55.1 percent/45.9 percent) better at closing deals they forecast. This ability may be the reason for the CMM companies' higher quota attainment when compared with the other companies. However, as you'll see in the sections that follow, this is just the beginning. There appear to be multiple benefits favoring CMM companies.

In further analyzing forecast accuracy, the study drilled down more deeply into the specific percentage of deals. In the general population, at best, 90 percent of all deals did not close as forecast (Figure 5-3). In other words, the close date, deal size, or some other component changed from the initial forecast description to the final booking (if it came in at all).

Given this level of "visibility" into the pipeline, there is little for companies to utilize in their planning efforts. At the highest range of accuracy

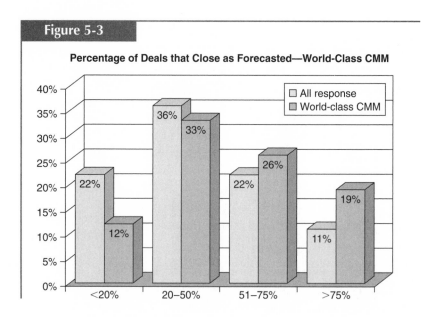

Figure 5-3

Percentage of Deals that Close as Forecasted—World-Class CMM

(>75 percent), the CMM firms' ratings came in as forecast 19 percent of the time, significantly higher than the general population, and performed almost 20 percent better in the next level of accuracy (51–75 percent as defined).

At the other end of the scale, where deals close as forecast less than one in five times, the CMM companies performed nearly twice as well (22 percent versus 12 percent). In other words, CMM companies are more accurate more of the time and less accurate less of the time. These differences are significant when applied to the gross revenue dollars of your company.

Virtuous Versus Vicious Cycle

It's important to note that these are trends and do not necessarily dictate that with a CMM initiative in place, all performance measures will improve. However, it is not a major leap to imagine that going through the discipline of defining customer messages/stories and creating a culture that enforces and reinforces a consistent approach will derive long-term performance gains. Jim Collins labeled this the "flywheel effect": small but ongoing movements gather momentum to show large gains in sum over time.

This phenomenon is reflected in the following two charts showing the percentage of presentations that ultimately resulted in a sale (Figure 5-4) and the percentage of proposals that close.

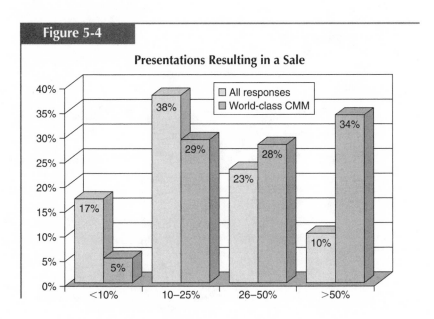

Figure 5-4

Presentations Resulting in a Sale

Past research shows ample evidence that when salespeople are left to their own devices, they will create market messages that may or may not be effective. When a CMM program is in place, and everyone is doing the same thing, organizations learn quickly. If the message is appropriate/successful, people use it. Word gets around. Conversely, if the message misses the mark, everyone knows and fixes it on their own.

Most firms in the survey indicated that the majority of their presentations are still conducted with clients face-to-face. This not only entails a significant investment in time to prepare these presentations, but also often a noticeable travel expense to meet with the prospect. Optimizing performance in this category can improve top-line revenue and bottom-line margins by reducing costs.

If the above benefits are true for optimizing the effectiveness of giving presentations, then they are even more so when you consider the more involved and difficult task of creating effective proposals.

The vast majority of the sales organizations we have talked to in the past two years have repeatedly stressed the fact that the days of the "casual purchase" (buyers making quick decisions to acquire a product or service without considering other options) have been reduced significantly, if not totally. To close business in today's world where purchases are scrutinized more than ever before, a solid business proposal must be crafted for the prospect. As seen in Figure 5-5, CMM appears to again have a noticeable impact on success rates.

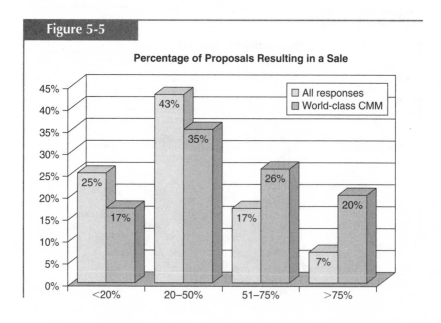

Figure 5-5

Percentage of Proposals Resulting in a Sale

- All responses
- World-class CMM

	<20%	20–50%	51–75%	>75%
All responses	25%	43%	17%	7%
World-class CMM	17%	35%	26%	20%

For many companies, generating proposals is a labor-intensive task involving not just sales but F&A, R&D, marketing, legal, customer support, etc. Having low hit rates impacts the effectiveness of not just sales, but many other functional areas. In the above chart, if a company were able to shift from column 1 to 2, 2 to 3, or 3 to 4, all other things being equal, the impact on revenues would be huge.

Again, the non-CMM companies saw much larger percentages of their proposal efforts resulting in a low percentage of hits: 24 percent were successful less than one in five times.

Whichever end of the scale you're experiencing, the flywheel is gaining momentum. Whether your presentations and proposals have good or poor returns, this reinforcing phenomenon is at work.

If good, you'll experience a "virtuous cycle" of continuously improving messaging, presenting, and proposing successes. If poor, the more energy you put in, the more energy will be required to sort through conflicting messages as they play out in your proposals and presentations, thus perpetuating a "vicious cycle" of decreasing returns.

Compounding Benefits

Having looked at overall performance and new business acquisition efforts, let's turn our attention to those areas that are generally the least additional cost, and often the highest additional profit: up-selling and cross-selling and avoiding excessive discounting. The differences between the sales population as a whole and the CMM subset can be seen here.

Cross-selling can take one of two forms. It can either mean adding additional products and/or services to an initial order, or penetrating additional departments or divisions of a customer. Up-selling generally means increasing an initial order with a higher-value solution. For example, a salesperson might convince a client that a $100 test kit should be upgraded to the $175 version because it has higher reliability, significantly faster response time, and longer shelf life. Up-selling could also be interpreted as calling higher within the buying organization, but this is not generally the definition.

As Figure 5-6 dramatically illustrates, the flywheel is now spinning at a much higher rate—for good or ill depending on the type of sales organization. The world-class CMM respondents effectively cross-sell and up-sell accounts almost three-quarters of the time.

By contrast, all other respondents miss out in this lucrative arena. More than one in five execute at a "Poor" level and at an "Average" level nearly two times in five. These are accounts in which you've already passed the

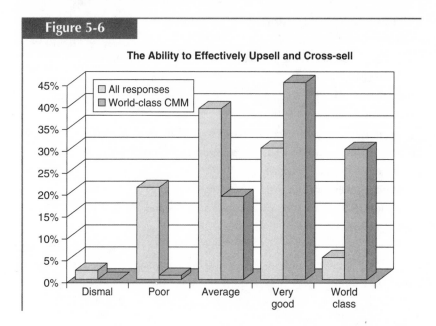

Figure 5-6

The Ability to Effectively Upsell and Cross-sell

major hurdles of gaining awareness, exploring needs, and overcoming objections. They've already bought something from your company, or decided to do so. These are your best potential accounts, and failing to properly leverage them can have a significant impact on your overall sales performance.

A second area of profit contribution is simply not giving margin away; a discount not given falls straight to the bottom line. This has historically been an issue in sales. It was once reported that 90 percent of sales reps offer a discount without being asked.

While Figure 5-7 shows that across sales organizations as a whole, the trend toward excessive discounting is still prevalent, world-class CMM companies show a significant improvement in this critical sales performance.

Compare the world-class companies with the sales population as a whole in the category of "Poor" at their ability to sell value and avoid excessive discounting. Here the difference is striking.

Our research shows that salespeople tend to discount because they do not know how to justify the price. Simply giving them the appropriate conversations and messages when they are challenged by a buyer can have a significant impact on curbing this trend.

Selling value is not new, but it is news to see such dramatic differences. Although correlation does not necessarily directly imply a cause-and-effect relationship, in this particular metric, you can draw a straight line from

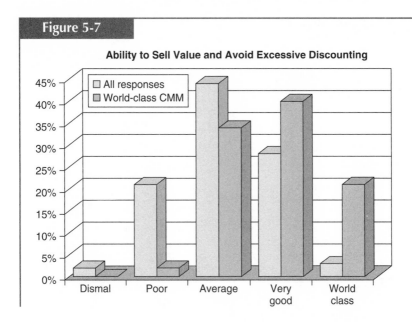

Figure 5-7

Ability to Sell Value and Avoid Excessive Discounting

consistent customer messaging to selling value—because consistent customer messaging, in part, means consistently delivering the right value statements. The results are reflected in the charts above and on each company's bottom line.

Selling the New Stuff

Another area of high potential is selling all products (this is partially covered by cross-selling), especially new products. When looking at their sales results, one manufacturer discovered that its reps were generating over 85 percent of the firm's revenues from regularly selling only 8 of 83 products. Worse, they were selling essentially none of their latest product line.

This is a double whammy for companies because familiar products, if successful, have most likely attracted competitive offerings, which in turn will diminish market share and profit margins. At the same time, new products need to launch quickly to recoup development costs, minimize expenses of educating buyers, and beat the competition to acquiring market share.

Once again, in this very important area, world-class CMM companies cash in while the majority of respondents trail. Previous research shows that reps need clear, concise messages to feel comfortable introducing new products. Even though, and maybe especially because, reps already have rapport and

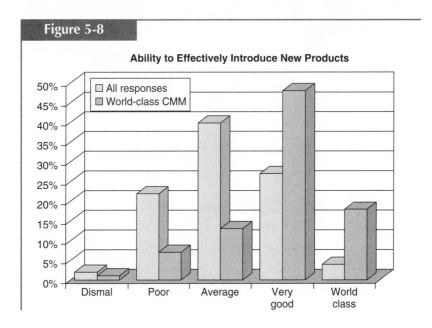

Figure 5-8

Ability to Effectively Introduce New Products

- All responses
- World-class CMM

credibility with customers, they don't want to appear ignorant or incompetent when discussing something new.

What does this mean to your company? If you are part of the gray bars in Figure 5-8, you're likely frustrated by your sales force's inability to get new products to market. This frustration is often exacerbated if you feel you have a better solution. Often, companies that pride themselves on their product prowess berate their competitors as being simply "marketing companies."

Key Chapter Take-Aways

From the CSO Insights survey:

- CMM companies outdistanced others in **quota achievement by 25 percent.**
- **Win rates for CMM firms are 20 percent higher** than the general population of sales forces.
- **Forecast accuracy** is significantly higher for world-class CMM organizations.
- The CMM group shows **3.4X improvement in return on effort in the highest-yield category of proposals** resulting in a close.
- CMM companies are **three times as successful in the highest-proposal win** category.

- CMM companies are significantly **more successful at up-selling and cross-selling.**
- World-Class CMM companies **avoid excessive discounting by a factor of 5.**
- CMM companies are significantly **more effective at introducing new products.**

If you are looking to make an impact on sales effectiveness like we just described, you've picked up the right book. The next section details the practical approaches and practices associated with Customer Message Management. It can serve as a handbook to creating and delivering a "world-class" CMM initiative.

SECTION TWO

CMM IN PROCESS: A TRAINING HANDBOOK

CHAPTER 6

SETTING UP A CMM PROJECT PLAN AND TEAM

The Customer Message Management approach is being used by world-class companies and market leaders such as Caterpillar, AmerisourceBergen, SAS Institute, ADP, and others to increase marketing's impact on sales success. We will be sharing examples, best practices gleaned from our experiences working with these companies throughout this section of the book.

This second section of the book is designed to be a literal handbook for implementing the CMM process within your organization. It's our intention to give you the ingredients for introducing the concept and executing a Phase One Project. The results of that introductory project, and the experience you gain, should prepare you to present a broader business case for turning CMM into an enterprise mission—which happens to be section three of this book.

In this chapter we will provide an overview of the CMM project plan. We'll then break each section of the plan into their respective chapters, which will provide detailed descriptions of each step, the associated activities, resource requirements, tools, templates, and best-practice examples.

Chapter 7: Building a Message Map The Message Map establishes the critical conversations that your company needs to have with customers. The first step in building a map is making important decisions about how your company will drive revenue in the upcoming 6–12 months, and the key

Figure 6-1

CMM Project Plan Overview

Develop a Message Map	Cross-Functional Messaging Workshop	Message Writing and Validation	Sales-Cycle-Relevant Deliverable Design
Chapter 7	Chapter 8	Chapter 9	Chapter 10

conversations or messages that your sales channels will need to communicate to meet your revenue goals.

This session is conducted in stages with executives, sales and marketing management, and cross-functional teams who are responsible for positioning and selling solutions. In Chapter 7 we will work through the critical Message Map decisions with questions and examples so you can facilitate these executive discussions.

- **Company goals review.** Determine exactly where your company needs to drive revenue in the upcoming year.
- **Go-to-market assessment.** Confirm the target segments and decision-makers, along with defining the selling channels that need to communicate your messages to customers.
- **Solution messaging process.** Build a cross-product silo, cross-functional messaging function that can spearhead the CMM process and facilitate critical company decision-making.
- **Sales performance audit.** Define the depth of messaging needed to successfully tell your story, and the corresponding competency required by your sales channels.

Deliverable: A Message Map that is customized to reflect your target markets, decision-makers, their business needs, and the depth of messaging required by your sales channels.

Chapter 8: Cross-Functional Messaging Workshop   In Chapter 8 we will provide you with a detailed CMM Business Story Worksheet that you will complete in the workshop to capture sufficient detail to circulate for review and validation.

This workshop is typically a two-day exercise with cross-functional resources (sales, services, marketing) to drive out critical components of customer-focused messaging. These components include the following:

- **Opportunity development** (helping identify and determine audience needs). A prospect becomes an "opportunity" when a salesperson can identify and qualify a legitimate business objective and related requirements (pains) that can be solved by your company. This exercise is critical to gaining consensus around the most common opportunities because these business needs will serve as the platform for creating your customer messaging content.
- **Solution mapping** (aligning corresponding capabilities). Working with a buyer to create and visualize a solution requires that your

company proactively map your corresponding capabilities (products, services, programs) to each of the previously identified business needs. In this exercise it is imperative to build an "Application Description" that shows how the decision-maker can *use* the capabilities to solve the specific business needs on the way to helping achieve their objectives.

- **Contextual value:** (build value statements). Value can only be proposed within the customer's context—specifically, the value a decision-maker can achieve by solving the business need with your company's capability. Here it is critical to describe the *business, operational, and financial* impact of your company's capability within this customer context.

Deliverable: Complete and edited workshop report containing each of the elements described above for each key business objective and related business need.

Chapter 9: Message Development and Validation   This step is a validation of the customer messaging components that will drive more consistent, high-quality sales communications.

In Chapter 9 we will provide exercises for creating CMM content and best-practice examples of completed worksheets to give you a benchmark for building your own content that will stand up in the field and in front of customers.

- **Message development.** The CMM Business Story Worksheet guides the creation of all the necessary messaging components needed to help salespeople conduct a consultative conversation and equip them with supporting communications tools.
- **Content validation.** Validation is critical to the CMM process. Making sure the messaging is useful in the field and in front of customers is part of this step in the project.

Deliverable: Completed CMM Business Story Worksheets for each of the identified business needs.

Chapter 10: Sales-Cycle-Relevant Deliverable Design   This is typically a two-day exercise to determine the most appropriate and useful marketing communications, training, coaching, and sales support tools. The key is to understand the ideal customer buying process and related steps of the sales cycle, and then determine the key applications for CMM content support, including the anatomy of the most appropriate deliverables.

In Chapter 10 we will provide an approach for creating new collateral tools—emphasizing the CMM content components used and their approximate layout—that support the sales cycle. Also, we will discuss the various potential delivery/distribution strategies leveraging today's marketing and sales intranet and automation technologies.

- **Map the customer buying process and best practice sales cycle.** This is a facilitated discussion with sales leaders and trainers, as well as the CMM project team. For each step in the cycle you will identify the objectives for each key "meaningful interaction" where a salesperson has a particular conversation or presentation with a customer, and/or needs to provide a specific type of document that advances the process toward a close. In each case, you will identify the specific content and structure of each conversation and deliverable.

- **Construct the coaching and collateral hierarchy.** The same joint sales and marketing participants will determine the tools, types, and variations required to build a library of conversation, presentation, and documentation templates. This includes roughly designing the layout of the tools, the content to be used, graphics required, and other related detail.

- **Link content to the sales conversations and collaterals.** Demonstrate how the CMM business stories and supporting content can be leveraged in each circumstance. Then determine the best way to equip salespeople for an intelligent, consultative conversation, as well as enable them to produce high-quality documented presentations of the information. A CMM Selling Kit includes a variety of internal coaching and customer-facing communications tools that can be used to help salespeople ramp-up and prepare to deliver more consistent, high-quality, customer-focused sales conversations, presentations, and documentation.

- **Determine the best deployment and access strategy.** Working with the marketing and CMM project team, content management resources, and necessary IT contacts to determine a useful content delivery strategy, including how the content is stored, maintained, and made accessible to salespeople in a way that works the way they work.

Deliverable: Summary of your company's preferred sales cycle/process, including step-by-step descriptions of the objectives, required support, and recommended CMM Selling Kit.

Are You Ready?

Customer Message Management—like most successful new processes—is 20 percent strategy and 80 percent implementation. So the question remains: Are you ready? Is your organization ready?

We could talk about all of the critical components to successful change management: getting buy-in at all levels, involving the people who will be affected by the change, honest reporting on progress, using both the formal communication network and the company grapevine. While all of those things are important, and we'll blend them into the discussion, there are some unique issues around CMM. Let's tackle them right away.

It's one thing to give lip service to the importance of integrating marketing and sales. Most marketers believe in the principles of CMM. Yet when it comes to implementation, they treat the initiative as a silo'd venture—continuing the same practices that have led to disparate processes, ineffective messages, and general marketing irrelevance.

Figure 6-2

Launching a Successful CMM Project

Very Successful CMM Implementations	Less Successful CMM Implementations
Top-down agreement that integrating sales and marketing processes is key to company success	Marketing/management belief that downstream branding and sales messaging are "not our job"
Clear implementation timeframe and target for messaging and use of messages	Agree with the CMM principles, but have not selected a market target—where to impact first
Decision to institutionalize the CMM process	Decision to develop content; process is secondary
Involvement of others responsible for integrated marketing strategy—vision for leveraging the process and messages across many touch-points	Self-protective or competitive vision for using new messages in one tool or medium—inability to leverage the Message Map to other touch-points
Identify and support CMM leadership; many companies create a new corporate position or role	Treat CMM as another project on someone's plate; not seen as a corporate process or asset

CMM Readiness Checklist

We assume you're reading Section Two of this book because (1) you want to get started on a CMM implementation, (2) you're trying to determine if CMM makes sense for your company, or (3) someone told you to read it.

Regardless, let's find out where you can make the biggest impact. Use the worksheets below to start the dialogue about initiating CMM in your company.

This might feel like the first step in a self-improvement program. Try it with your team. Work through it with management. Use the definitions and statistics from Section One to introduce CMM and its potential impact on sales and marketing organizations.

Avoid preparing the group with the answers that you'd like to hear—leading the witness to your priorities. Use the discussion to determine whether or not your organization—both up to management and down to the implementers—are united in making a change.

The problem usually narrows down to one of the following five issues. We encourage you to adjust and prioritize these five issues based on your company's goals.

Priority:____ We need to differentiate our real value versus competitors'.

The amount of business information that your customers sift through to make business decisions doubles every 1,100 days. It's no wonder they have a hard time distinguishing among top competitors that look more or less the same.

- Product value props make us appear like separate companies.
- Value props presume too much about what customers value.
- Value messages are not in the customer's context.

Figure 6-3

Is There a Problem?

- My role is _____.
- I think we have a marketing and sales alignment problem because _____
_____.
- The challenges that could prevent us from correcting this problem are _____
_____.
- The company goals or projects that will suffer most if we don't correct the problem are _____
_____.

Priority:____ We need to elevate from feature to solution selling.

Your products and services are not a "solution" until a prospect says so. The intersection between customer profile, business need, and corresponding capability is where you can build a solution in the eye of the customer.

- Despite sales training investments, we are still selling products.
- Product "silos" prevent us from a real solution sell.
- Our "solutions" are just a mass list of products and services.

Priority:____ We need to build sales-ready support and tools.

Statistics indicate that up to 90 percent of the content created for sales support goes unused in the field, and that over 97 percent of campaigns are irrelevant to the customers they were intended to attract. In a highly competitive marketplace, this is one place where a small change could make a big difference.

- We're not sure what sales uses or needs to sell.
- Sales creates maverick tools despite what marketing does.
- Our messaging is at the 30,000-foot level—not at the point of sale.

Priority:____ We need to improve performance of our sales reps/channels.

Most career salespeople have been trained on some form of consultative, solution selling. Most sales update and launch training is designed to "gain mindshare" on specific products. Unfortunately, only your best people (about 10 percent of any sales team) will be able to put the solution puzzle together—having the right conversations and positioning your best answer.

Getting trained on a sales approach—without having the questions to ask and story to tell—is like having a race car with no fuel. It doesn't go where we need it to go. Getting trained repeatedly on products and features—without the context of the sales process—doesn't help them have the confident, competent conversations that can move the sales process forward.

- Solution selling doesn't work if people don't know what to say.
- Sales training is aligned with products, not with the customer buying process.
- Salespeople position what they know—and what they are compensated to sell.

Priority:____ We need to create "one voice" to customers across touch-points.

The number of departments and people inside companies who create customer messages seems to be growing, as does the number of channels to deliver that content. Conflicting themes, approaches, and one-off, self-styled customer communications have companies competing with themselves to deliver a coherent story.

- Our internal groups compete to deliver our value story.
- Lack of shared messaging process results in inconsistent, conflicting messages.
- We don't agree internally on our customer buying process.

CMM NOTE

Indicators of a Sales and Marketing Disconnect

1. *Marketing is seen as the back end of product development, not the front end of the sales success.*

2. *Marketing budget is weighted toward up-front promotions and awareness campaigns.*

3. *Marketing and sales do not have shared performance objectives and metrics.*

4. *Market segmentation differs from the way sales is organized and incented.*

5. *Messaging is based on products, not on needs-based conversations with buyers.*

6. *Marketing has no idea if, when, and how messages are used by sales with customers.*

7. *The marketing/sales portal is a growing cesspool of unused and outdated information.*

8. *Sales training is focused on product knowledge and gaining sales mindshare.*

Refine the CMM Target

After you or your team has agreed that there is a sales and marketing disconnect, and that it is important enough to merit attention, then refine your target.

- **Business goal.** Restate your company's messaging goal or problem. Link it to something that your organization cares about—ideally something specifically linked to revenue generation. What is the upside of solving the problem, or the downside of not solving it?

- **Challenges.** Restate your challenges. What would prevent your organization from solving the problem or achieving the business goal?
- **Focus.** Narrow your company goal down to a messaging "target"—a key conversation that your company needs to have with a particular industry segment or type of buyer to find, keep, or up-sell customers and prospects.

  - How is this message currently created? What's right and wrong with that process?
  - Who is the message supposed to influence? Why? What is the role of that audience in the buying process? Do your sales channels currently communicate with that audience?
  - Who or what delivers this message today? When and how is the message used in the customer buying cycle? What's right and wrong with that process?

How Big Is the Elephant?

As the saying goes—it's easier to eat an elephant if you do it piece by piece. One of our customers decided to swallow the whole beast, despite our recommendation to the contrary. So they removed all marketing collateral from the field. What did sales do? They copied, pasted, fabricated, cajoled, begged, borrowed, and stole what they needed to get the job done so they could close deals.

A top salesperson once told us that "good salespeople are like water. They will flow down the path of least resistance to get to the finish line." In other words, they'll get the job done—ethically, but by following the most expedient path to the goal.

In determining the scope of your CMM initiative, focus on getting the process in place and implementing it on a manageable—yet visible and meaningful—target. Involve other people who are part of integrated marketing communications. Create a vision around the process. Before you know it, someone on that team will ask to leverage the messages in another way—in sales training, on your Web site, in a trade show, in other collaterals, in call center scripts, etc. The more consistently you inform and support multiple touch-points from the same Message Map, the more benefit your company will derive in terms of efficient process and effective value messaging to your markets and customers.

In our American Marketing Association training programs, we work with B2B and B2C companies of all sizes—from marketing teams with one person to organizations with hundreds of people and large, approved budgets. We often hear this plea: "I can only affect my scope of influence—and it's pretty small." Your scope of influence might be a particular type of collateral, a part of the marketing process, a specific product, or a specific industry. *Big or small, the CMM process holds true.* By bringing customer focus to customer messaging, and implementing a practical, repeatable process, you have the opportunity to increase marketing's relevance on sales—and build an example and a vision.

Roles, Tasks, and Preparation

Some companies implement CMM with a team of one. You can do it. Obviously the bigger the company, and the more business units and products, the more complex the knot that has to be untangled. So a wider advisory and talent pool is needed.

We'll categorize the project resources according to three project phases: strategy, development, and implementation (Figures 6-4 through 6-6). For

Figure 6-4

CMM Strategy—Establishing Vision, Scope, Metrics, and Resources

CMM Strategy		
Role	*Tasks*	*Preparation*
Executive visionary	• Manage CMM metrics • Promote CMM process • Select CMM target project	Understand the CMM principles and potential impact defined in Section One of this book
CMM consultant	• Develop CMM strategy • Advise organization on CMM • Implement the CMM process	Understand CMM principles, potential impact, process, and tools defined in Sections One and Two of this book
Sales and Marketing management	• Advise on marketing and sales targets and performance metrics • Ensure alignment with marketing strategy, sales incentives, territory/account assignments, etc. • Allocate appropriate resources	Understand the CMM principles and potential impact; process steps and resources

Figure 6-5

CMM Development—Creating Customer-Focused Messages

CMM Development		
Role	*Tasks*	*Preparation*
Messaging facilitator	• Organize and lead Messaging Workshops with sales/marketing • Conduct Sales Process Alignment Workshop to determine sales-ready deliverables • Validate messages with sales, marketing (and customers)	Practice conducting a Messaging Workshop as defined in Section Two; modify and customize the workshop tools for your company
CMM consultant	• Develop Message Map and sample deliverables based on Sales Process Alignment Workshop	Coordinate Message Mapping with facilitator to ensure that Messaging Workshop drives out the right level of content
Sales advisory team	• Participate in Messaging Workshop and Sales Process Alignment	Prepare for workshops given an assignment by CMM consultant
Marketing team	• Participate in Messaging Workshop and Sales Process Alignment • Conduct collateral audit as part of Sales Process Alignment • Provide product and company expertise in writing messages	Prepare for workshop given an assignment by CMM consultant
Message writer	• Attend workshops to take notes and gather information needed to write messages • Work with marketing team, facilitator, CMM consultant to write and validate messages	Read "Writing for CMM" chapter in Section Two of this book Before the Messaging Workshop, use the Message Map to write a "test story" as an example for the Workshop

Figure 6-6

CMM Implementation—Using Messages to Support Selling

CMM Implementation		
Role	*Tasks*	*Preparation*
CMM consultant	• Manage message use • Determine message technology requirements, if available • Plan message expansion	Read Section Three of this book to see how other companies have used messages in various integrated communications
Creative / layout	• Create and standardize templates to use messaging content	Meet with CMM consultant to understand the rigor of a Message Map and how content can be leveraged across various touchpoints
Marketing communications	• Plan consistent integration of messaging in marketing collaterals	Read appropriate chapters in Section Three of this book to see how others have used messages in collaterals
Product and sales training	• Plan integration of messaging into product and sales training	Read appropriate chapters in Section Three of this book to see how others have used messages in training
Web site team	• Plan integration of messaging into Web site (or sales portal)	Read appropriate chapters in Section Three of this book to see how others have used messages in Web sites
Corporate communications / brand communications	• Plan integration of messaging into corporate communications	Read appropriate chapters in Section Three of this book to see how others have used messages to promote brand
Proposal team	• Plan integration of messaging into proposals, RFPs, and RFIs	Read appropriate chapters in Section Three of this book to see how others have used messages in proposals

each role, think about the person or group that is best positioned to handle the tasks, and best able to adapt and institutionalize the process. Note that one person may play multiple roles.

CMM Metrics

In determining organizational readiness, you will discover your company's business goals and associated metrics. By mapping the sales process to the marketing approach, you will have insight into messaging gaps that translate to significant sales opportunities.

Chapter Five provides metrics and results of world-class CMM companies. The companies that we work with generally select one or two measurable results for the initial CMM implementation, and discuss longer-term metrics as part of the CMM vision.

Below are some metrics used by our customers:

Qualitative

- Sales satisfaction with marketing/marketing support
- Sales confidence in selling or promoting specific solutions/ products
- Perceived marketing relevance to revenue generation
- Content re-usability/less redundant effort

Quantitative—Shorter term

- Sales ramp-up time after launch (measured by testing/ certification)
- Sales message competency (measured by testing/ certification)
- Revenue per salesperson
- Quota achievement
- Cost of sale (by region, district, other)
- Days to close (or days to another key milestone in your sales process)
- Win rate/proposal win rate/demo win rate
- Forecast accuracy
- Up-selling and cross-selling
- Reduced discounting

Figure 6-7

CMM Baseline Assessment

	Strongly agree	Agree	Neutral	Disagree	Strongly disagree
1. At the end of the day, the positioning of our offerings boils down to the words and phrases salespeople use when they talk to buyers.					
2. A small percentage of our salespeople are able to converse effectively with decision-makers.					
3. Our messages are positioned consistently across our various channels to buyers.					
4. A sales cycle begins once a buyer shares a business problem, need, or goal with a seller.					
5. The only person who can call something a "solution" is the buyer.					
6. By necessity, most of our company's training for salespeople is product-oriented.					
7. Training introduces applications, but it's up to our salespeople to determine how the products are used day-to-day by customers.					
8. Creating the organization's "core messaging" is the most important task for any company.					
9. Marketing is the front end of the sales process, not the back end of product development.					

(Continued)

Figure 6-7

CMM Baseline Assessment (Continued)

	Strongly agree	Agree	Neutral	Disagree	Strongly disagree
10. Most of the time, the customer's decision to buy our brand is made at the point of sale.					
11. Between 50- and 90-percent of the material created by marketing to support sales is never used by salespeople.					
12. Most marketing collateral is NOT intended for use during the sales call, but rather to create awareness/interest before the call and to provide information/proposals after the call.					
13. Automated chaos is still chaos.					
14. Marketing doesn't know what it takes to sell our solutions to buyers in our markets.					
15. Sales doesn't understand our solutions well enough to position them with buyers.					

Key Chapter Take-Aways

- Most of us **have a lot of data,** but we're challenged to do something meaningful with it. Sure, it's great information—representing a big dollar investment. But how are you using it to make sales?
- Customer Message Management—like most successful new processes—is 20 percent strategy and 80 percent implementation. It's **a repeatable, manageable process** that works, regardless of your company or department size.

- A key pitfall in CMM implementation is providing lip service to the principles, but treating the initiative as a silo'd venture—continuing the same practices that have led to disparate processes, ineffective messages, and general marketing irrelevance.
- **Focus on getting the process in place** and implementing it on a manageable—yet visible and meaningful—target. Create a vision around the process. The more consistently you inform and support multiple touch-points from the same Message Map, the bigger the benefit to your company.
- You can implement CMM with a team of 1 or 100. The bigger the company, and the more business units and products, the more complex the knot that has to be untangled—so a wider **advisory and talent pool** is needed.

In the next chapter we will work through the process of developing a Message Map, and aligning messages to sales process.

CHAPTER 7

BUILDING A MESSAGE MAP

Some ideas gain steam quickly. Since we first started talking about a Message Map in 2000, we've learned that the concept is clearly a hot topic. Putting structure to a traditionally unstructured messaging process leads to untold efficiencies and consistencies.

Here's the problem: People have a tendency to make things complicated. We've seen various marketing maps and processes that require project tracking software, IT gurus, and tagged data reports just to get the big idea across to the average human being. Nothing will kill a good idea faster than an overly complex, unsustainable implementation.

Our Message Map approach is deceptively simple. It's easily communicated, practical, and manageable. We believe that the map can and must be simple, because the problem we are tackling—customer messaging—is not.

The CMM Message Map gives your company a common language for message development and use, and a logical series of five steps that both marketing and sales can embrace (see Figure 7-1).

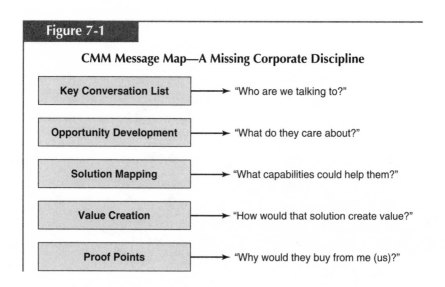

Figure 7-1

CMM Message Map—A Missing Corporate Discipline

Key Conversation List	→ "Who are we talking to?"
Opportunity Development	→ "What do they care about?"
Solution Mapping	→ "What capabilities could help them?"
Value Creation	→ "How would that solution create value?"
Proof Points	→ "Why would they buy from me (us)?"

Selling is a series of conversations. Your best salespeople know this. In fact, they tend to ignore corporate messages and other 30,000-foot campaigns in lieu of having the right conversations with customers.

The Message Map is a template that enables your company to consistently and repeatedly build the conversations you need to have with key decision-makers in your target markets—whether those conversations take place with a call center rep, direct salesperson, channel partner or distributor, or even a self-service web interaction.

If you asked your best salespeople what they think about in preparation for an important customer conversation, they would tell you something like this:

Buyer Roles	Who will I call or meet with today? What are their roles in the buying process?
Buyer Goals	What are their business goals? What's going on in their company or in the industry that matters most to them? Why would they even give me 30 minutes of their time? If they are a current customer, what goals did we address in the solution that they bought? Are they happy with the results?
Solution	What can I discuss that could help them solve their business problems? How can I talk about our capabilities without sounding like a product brochure or demo dolly? How can I work with them to build a solution in their mind's eye?
Value	What value could they get by using this solution? How will it specifically address their business goals? How much of this can be quantified? Why would they buy this from us versus our competitor?
Proof	How can we demonstrate our ability to solve this problem? How can we prove or substantiate our value? Why would they believe us?

In fact, the first four points are *often used by sales managers in a post-call review* with their sales reps. In some cases, this process is taught specifically as part of solutions-oriented selling methodologies. Whether this thought process is written down or not, it's essentially the same from company to company as they become more consultative sellers—because it's been field-proven to work.

Do most marketers follow and feed this deceptively simple consultative conversation format when we develop our messages? Or are we beholden to building messages from the product down or company out?

Here are some of the challenges that we see over and over again, things that prevent the simple from becoming sanctioned:

- **Lack of Consensus on Buyer Roles.** The organization doesn't agree on the target industries, markets, or roles of decision-makers in the buying process. Sales may be organized and incented around a completely different set of market definitions than marketing.

- **No Clear Understanding of Buyer Goals.** Because organizations usually operate in product silos, it's easy to manipulate and shape-change product features until they resemble customer needs.

- **Inability to Create True Solutions.** With individual P&L, product groups have little incentive to cross product lines and promote their combined "best answer" for a given buyer goal. Sales reps want to tell a story that makes sense to the customer, and they want to focus on three or four capabilities as the best answer to the problem. They don't want to spray and pray.

- **Valueless Value Propositions.** Value propositions tend to be presumptuous—they presume value by stating a generic benefit for every feature. This is really only a glorified functional performance description because value statements don't exist until a solution maps to a buyer goal. No sales rep will remember all of those generic benefit statements anyway.

- **Hard-to-Find Proof.** It's like Goldilocks looking for the perfect porridge in the Three Bears' cottage. Sales reps always tell us that there are too many case studies and approved customer stories to find and sort through, or too few relevant and current proofs. But it's never just right.

Considerations for a Message Map

The Message Map mimics the critical conversations that your company needs to have with customers. In this step of the process, you'll need to start making critical decisions about your Message Map. These decisions are based on four things:

1. **Company Goals Review.** What areas of the company need better messaging behind them in order to drive revenue? Which market

segments do you want to protect or expand? From which solution groups or areas would you like to derive more growth?

2. **Go-to-Market Assessment.** Which touch-points and selling channels are critical for communicating your messages to the target customers? How much of the sales cycle is driven by self-service contacts and information gathering such as the web? Where are field sales representatives and specialists critical to closing the deal? Are you organized, trained, and incented to support the company's revenue goals?

3. **Solution Messaging Process.** Do your best answers to a market segment's key challenges cross various product or functional silos in the organization? Do these business units work well together? Will you need to create a cohesive messaging approach to create solutions among currently or typically disparate groups? At what level do we need to coordinate this activity?

4. **Sales Performance Audit.** How prepared is your sales force to help drive the kind of solutions business you want to create? What depth of messaging is needed to equip the field to successfully tell your story? What kind of corresponding competencies and training are required by your sales channels?

As the CMM consultant within your department or organization, you can help drive these four important discussions that will build a foundation for the Message Map. Since the Message Map is the "true north" for your CMM compass, it needs to be right on.

Everything we do from this point will build from the Message Map. So let's work through each of these important discussions and describe who should be involved, and the collaborative decisions that you will need to take for your Message Map.

Company Goals Review: Where does the Company Want to Drive Revenue?

Have This Conversation With

1. Sales management/VP Sales
2. Business development/new business
3. Marketing management/VP Marketing

Customer Message Management must be driven, and guided, by your company's revenue-generating goals and activities. Where is your company directing the field to sell? Which new markets do they want to crack? Which new offerings do they want to aggressively leverage in the market? Which industries segments are you vigorously trying to defend? In which competitive categories are you trying to grab share? Are there geographic segments or vertical industries in which you need to make a concerted effort?

Setting up a successful CMM initiative requires that you align and support one or more of these revenue-generating goals. Here's a list of discussion questions you can use to uncover or confirm these goals with the executive team.

Discussion Questions:

1. What are this company's goals for driving new business this year? In which segments, or with which types of prospects? Which products or solutions will we emphasize to achieve this growth? What is the competitive landscape in these markets, and how do we stack up? Do we have any goals for increasing deal size?

2. Do we have goals for existing customer expansion or account penetration? Have we created any categories or identified any segments within our customers and targeted them for particular cross-sell or up-sell approaches? Have we identified the offerings we want to emphasize?

3. Do we have goals for existing customer retention, or contract renewals? Do we know which customers we need to target to ensure this? How are we addressing these "keep" activities with offerings, and our sales and marketing activities?

4. Are we planning to launch any new products or services for a significant revenue impact? Will we partner or merge with another company to expand our offerings? How will this position us competitively? Will it allow us to enter new categories we haven't been in before? Are both marketing and sales channels ready to absorb these updates and make the necessary revenue impact? How do we know?

5. Are we trying to reduce the cost of sales in order to drive more revenue? Are we looking to streamline our sales processes in specific ways: improved pipeline management, better resource utilization, increasing close rates? Will there be any significant changes in our sales channel, training, and support to make this happen?

Go-to-Market Assessment: Which Channels will Communicate the Messages?

Have This Conversation With

- Sales management/VP Sales
- Marketing management/VP Marketing
- Integrated marketing communications
- Solutions marketing
- Web team

Once you've established the company's revenue-generating goals, you then have to determine how the company plans to *actualize* these goals. This is often referred to as "go-to-market" strategy. It refers to the way your company will deploy its marketing and sales resources to achieve the stated revenue goals.

When it comes to aligning your CMM initiative with the company's go-to-market strategy, it is important to remember the key premise of Customer Message Management: *The majority of revenue generating impact occurs in one place—at the point of sales contact with the customer.*

Ultimately, you will need to develop and deliver messages that support selling conversations/dialogues with customer decision-makers in order to make your revenue goals a reality. Here's a list of questions you need to ask to further refine your CMM Message Map and ensure that it is aligned with the company's go-to-market strategy:

Discussion Questions:

1. Which market segments or industries are essential targets based on our company's revenue-generating goals?
2. For each segment or industry, who are the key decision-makers? What positions or roles do these decision-makers play in their organizations?
   a. User buyer?
   b. Financial buyer?
   c. Business buyer?
   d. Technical/IT buyer?
   e. C-level buyers?
   f. External consultants or other influencers?

3. For each key decision-maker, what are they trying to achieve? In other words, what keeps them up at night? What business impacts are they looking to create? How do we know?

4. Which marketing and sales channels communicate with these buyers today? What are we doing to segment our messages according to these buyers? Have we deployed messages at the point of sales contact with our company? Do our campaigns and events reflect this segmentation? Web site? Sales tools?

5. Which conversations are most comfortable for our sales team? Are we talking to the right buyers to achieve our revenue goals? In which conversations should we work to increase the competency and confidence of our sales team?

6. Are the salespeople compensated or incented relative to the company's revenue goals? Are they trained appropriately to deliver on the goals? What do our top-performing salespeople know or do differently than the average rep? As we look across the sales team, where would we like to see performance improvements? What's missing in their current competency set? Does our incentive program motivate the right behavior?

CMM NOTES

Segmentation's Law of Diminishing Returns

One of our customers believed that their segmentation was very complex. They felt that the messages needed to differ based on size of the customer's business (small, medium, large, enterprise); the type of buyer; and on regional differences (Southeast U.S., Midwest U.S., Northeast U.S., etc.). The resulting Message Map and exponential variations of content would have been a nightmare to develop and manage.

Just because you can "map" it doesn't make it the right thing to do. There's always a law of diminishing returns when it comes to targeting and segmenting messaging. In this case, when we peeled the onion, we found that the real variation was in the "proofs" used as part of the sale. While we needed to talk specifically to each buyer's needs, small- and medium-sized customers wanted to see case studies from similarly sized businesses. Large or enterprise customers needed proof points from other large or enterprise customers.

We were able to develop messaging to support key conversations with four types of decision-makers, each of whom had three to five business goals. We mapped

> *capabilities and value to the business goals of each decision-maker—so that the conversations were specific to those decision-makers. Then just proof points were plotted for the more detailed size and geographic segmentations.*
>
> *The reason for this is that the problems and solutions were almost completely portable across the segments. And we discovered that the most important thing this company's prospects really wanted to know was "What other companies have you done this for that look like me?" And "Who else in my area have you done this for?"*

Solution Messaging Process: How will cross-silo messaging occur in your organization?

Have This Conversation With

- Sales management/VP Sales
- Marketing management/VP Marketing
- Solutions marketing
- Sales training strategist

Salespeople have been trained to position and sell "solutions" for decades. Solution selling and consultative selling are not new concepts. For a top-performing salesperson, selling solutions means identifying the customer needs by asking good questions, and then mapping the "best answer" to those needs.

Often, this best answer is a combination of products, capabilities, programs, and services that crosses over organizational silos such as business units and individual product management responsibilities. Let's be honest: our Web sites, marketing communications, and sales tools and training—what we sell—are typically driven by individual products. But what customers are buying is an answer to a problem. And that best answer requires cross-silo or cross-functional messaging in order to help a salesperson build a solution in the mind's eye of the customer.

Here's the question: Do you want to leave it to the salesperson to look across your marketing and product silos to determine the best answer, and create customer-focused communications? Or do you want to more proactively organize and coordinate our silo'd activity in a cross-functional effort to equip more consultative solutions selling that meets the expectations of customers?

As a result, the Message Map is not just about choosing market segments, targeted decision-makers, and communications channels. It needs to include

Figure 7-2	

Solution Mapping—Company Products Vs. Customer Problems

What We Sell	What They Want to Do
Large format printers	Improve efficiency of communications in supply chain
Large format scanners	Reduce project management costs
Large format copiers	Increase quality control/reduce errors and re-work
Production printing continuous	Improve ability to respond to bids/tenders
Production printing cut sheet	Support just-in-time strategies and practices
Multi-function printers	Help us respond to customization and 1-1 needs
Production software	Improve storage, archive, and management
Document management software	We need better internal tracking and control processes
System integration software	Streamline printing capacity and workflow
Supplies	Upgrade the quality of our outputs at lower cost
Onsite staffing	Reduce resource (space and admin) costs
Consulting services	
Professional services	
Technical support	
Financing	

determining how and where *solution development* will occur within your organization.

Who can make cross-silo or cross-functional decisions about best answers for customer needs? Who has the skills, resources, and organizational structure to represent the customer at a solution level? Here are some discussion questions to help you determine the impact of solutions messaging on your Message Map:

Discussion Questions:

1. When a customer looks across our various touch-points (promotions, Web site, telesales, face-to-face sales, collaterals, proposals, retention communications, global marketing), can they easily get answers to their most pressing business problems? Even if they do, will they get a consistent message about the problems we solve, the way we solve them, and the value that other customers have derived from our solutions as they have contact with various touch-points? Where would a customer see inconsistency?

2. Are there situations where a customer or prospect might get conflicting best answers from our channels? How confident are we

that, when presented with a similar business problem by a similar prospect or customer, our salespeople will give the company's best answer? Do we struggle with our channels providing competitive best answers or solutions in addition to our own?

3. Who defines "solutions" within our organization? How are these solutions defined? Are they defined based upon customer needs, or are they a convenient bundling of assorted products? How do we define customer needs? Are the current customer needs reflections of true customer conversations, or are they marketing oriented (e.g., high quality, reliability, productivity, low cost)?

4. What mechanisms do we have in place to bridge gaps between product silos and to drive more cross-silo and cross-functional messaging? Do we have consensus on how we define our market segments and decision-makers? Do we have the capacity to work with sales and gain consensus around the truly predictable, repeatable customer needs that require a "best answer"?

5. Who can help determine our "best answer" solution in response to customer needs? Where does product marketing fit in? The sales rep? Our services group? Our proposal team? What's the best way to organize these subject-matter experts and referee the discussions?

Sales Performance Audit: What level of messaging competency is needed to tell your story?

Have This Conversation With

- Marketing implementation team
- Sales management
- Sales training
- Sales top performers

Your CMM Message Map is the template for creating your company's core customer conversation content. It's the guide for enabling all content creators to consistently build a customer-focused, value-selling story. It's a repeatable, sustainable structure for institutionalizing a corporate discipline and structured approach around the traditionally unstructured process of customer messaging.

One marketing VP told us that the "CMM Message Map brings rigor to messaging without rigor mortis." In other words, your company can now create messaging content—in the customer's context—that can be leveraged in various ways across the sales cycle.

Most of us are accustomed to developing messages that are used in single events such as an advertisement, a trade show graphic, a direct mail campaign, a brochure, a Web site, a presentation, or a proposal. These are stand-alone activities often disconnected from each other in their creation and delivery.

The reality is that a successful sales cycle is really a continuum of customer conversations that should build to a crescendo from the moment you identify a real customer need to the point where you close on a solution for solving that need.

The power of the Message Map is in aligning message creation, delivery, and management to the customer buying process. Specifically, providing messaging in the way salespeople need to use it, so they can fulfill their job of communicating messages to customers in the way customers want to consume it. (You may want to reread that last sentence to grasp the magnitude and implications of this change.)

As a result, our Message Map needs to reflect the customer conversation process, especially the "depth" of content needed by various sales channels to get deals done. It's one thing to provide better, more customer-focused messages and content to sales, but an entirely *more powerful and relevant position when we know when, how, by whom the messaging is used* to make decisions and drive revenue.

Discussion Questions:

1. Can we map the sales process (see sample sales process for reference)? Is it different for different types of sales? Who, from our company or partners, is involved at each point in the sales process?

2. Who are the decision-makers or influencers at each step of the sales process? What depth of messaging is necessary to support those conversations?

   a. Do we need to know current industry issues, trends, and hot buttons?

   b. What types of diagnostic questions are required to uncover, define, and confirm the business problem?

   c. How much detail do we need for each of the corresponding capabilities to communicate the impact and value of our solution on each of those problems?

   d. At what level do we need competitive information to paint a clear picture of differentiation and handle potential objections?

CMM NOTES

Mapping Messages to Sales Process

Mapping messaging requirements to the sales process is rarely done today, but is essential to Customer Message Management. This single exercise often brings great clarity to both sales and marketing. It also brings scope to your Message Map.

Most sales teams use some series of steps for forecasting and sales tracking. If your company uses sales force automation (SFA) or customer relationship management (CRM) software, then the steps are undoubtedly embedded in there. If not, find out how your sales team was trained—they may have been taught a forecasting process or sales methodology for your company.

The simple chart in Figure 7-3 is a good way to start the discussion with sales and marketing.

Figure 7-3

Mapping Message Requirements to Sales Process

Find an Opportunity	Identify the Needs	Develop a Solution	Create a Value Proposal	Negotiate and Close
Set up meeting with a decision maker; prepare yourself for the right level conversation	Identify business issues that the customer is willing to invest ($) in solving; talk to influencers	Map your "best answer" capabilities to the business issues to keep the sale focused and on track	Present measurable value and proof specific to how your solution solves the identified business issues	Propose a clear vision of the solution, cost, implementation, and metrics

↓   ↓   ↓   ↓   ↓

Map the messaging requirements for your sales cycle:
1. Key conversations at each step
2. Tools used before, during, or after
3. Redesign your marketing collaterals

---

e. What technical-, service-, or implementation-related information do we need to integrate as part of the solution-selling story?

f. What kinds of proof points are required to validate our proposed solutions—case studies, white papers, quotations, ROI assessments?

g. What types and levels of product demonstration are required to close a deal?

    h. What types of proposal documents and content are essential to closing a deal?

3. What mandated deliverables or customer communications are used to mark progress in a sales cycle? Where does the messaging and tools to support this come from? What other non-mandated support tools (coaching and customer-facing documents and presentations) are most often used at each step to help advance a sale? At which point in the sales process is the sales team having the biggest challenge moving the deal forward? Why? What type of information or sales support would be the most useful that isn't available now?

Interviewing Salespeople

Marketers often ask us what they should ask salespeople in order to understand the sales process. *"They won't talk to me,"* said one Marketing Communications Manager. "Or they tell me that everything is great, and that we should just keep doing what we've always done. But I know they're not using our stuff."

It's important to talk to sales in a way that reflects an understanding of how they work. Many salespeople have an ingrained perception that marketing "doesn't get what we do" and that marketing people "are doing their best, but it really doesn't make much of a difference to how I sell."

We can change this and become relevant to selling by first understanding what it really takes to get deals done—especially the conversations that occur with customers at the point of sale. The questions below will help you map the process that is formally in place to track opportunities in the pipeline, as well as the de facto process—in other words, your actual ("feet in the street") activities in working with accounts. These questions should also help you understand the types of sales support that move deals forward in the pipeline.

Sample Questions	To Help You Understand . . .
How long have you worked in this position for [COMPANY]? Where were you before that?	Experience working with the tools and issues or this organization
How long have you been in sales? How were your previous positions similar or different?	Experience working with different processes, solutions, markets, buyers
What is your current account package?	Number, types, and sizes of accounts

Sample Questions	To Help You Understand . . .
How often do you talk to each account? To the same or multiple people? For what reasons?	Level and frequency of contact, whether "live," phone, or email
Who else from [COMPANY] is in your accounts on a frequent basis? What roles do they play?	Actual team roles in supporting the customer, and coordination among roles
Would you say that your sales are more transactional, or more relationship management?	Number of selling interactions versus relationship-building interactions
Do you have different types of sales cycles—for example, a systems sale, or an integrated sale versus a component or single-service sale?	If different products, services, or solutions are sold differently, or in the same way to the same buyers following the same steps
What is different for each type of sales cycle—the duration, dollar amount, people involved?	Variation in requirements of sales cycles
Which sales cycle makes up the largest part of your pipeline? Are you trying to change that?	Priorities in selling various products and solutions; confidence in certain sales cycles
I'm sure you've been trained on a variety of sales methods. Which one stuck with you? Why?	Preference (or not) for particular method
How do you track sales activity in your pipeline? Is that required, or something unique that helps you determine your progress and next steps?	Whether individual, systems are used
It helps me understand the sales process if you walk me through a recent "win." Can we discuss a [sales cycle], starting from how you identified or created the opportunity through close?	"What happened next" for each type of sales cycle, who was involved/why, what information was needed, roadblocks that were overcome—discuss and map it
What would change if you were selling [sales cycle]? Can we discuss a similar "win"?	Comparison of different sales cycles—solutions sold, people involved, tools used
What are the most significant barriers or roadblocks in moving sales forward?	How they think they could sell more
What is most helpful as you move sales forward?	How they think they could sell more

(Continued)

Sample Questions	To Help You Understand . . .
What tools, information, or resources are part of your arsenal—something you can't do without?	Actual support (including people) used in selling—find out where each tool resides
For each of those tools, what does it accomplish in terms of moving your sales forward?	How tools are used—map to "create, cultivate, close" or similar process
What information or resources are always missing or difficult to get? Why?	What else is required in terms of information or resources
How do you think your customers view [COMPANY]? How does that help or hurt your?	Company personality from street level
How does the company message work with your customers? Do they buy it? Why or why not?	Company "story" resonance at street level
What types of business problems or challenges do you frequently hear from your customers?	Common customer needs—keep the focus on business issues, not complaints
What tools or information are most helpful as you create your message for each sale, if any?	How the message is created per customer
How do you establish "value" with the customer?	How value is built per customer
What are your biggest concerns about maintaining your existing accounts, if any?	Account maintenance opportunities
What are your biggest opportunities to grow your existing accounts? What would it take to do that?	Relationship up-sell opportunities
Where are your biggest opportunities to find new business? What would it take to do that?	Net new opportunities
How would you end this statement: "To help me sell more, I wish marketing would . . ."	Open-ended wish list discussion

Apply Decisions to Your Message Map

After having the discussions outlined in this chapter, you should have answers to these important decisions:

Company Goals Review: *Where your company is looking to drive revenue*
Significant revenue-generating activities for upcoming year: _____
Target market segments or industries for upcoming year: _____
Significant product launch or offering updates for the upcoming year: _____

Anticipated sales and marketing changes in upcoming year: _____

Go-to-Market Assessment: *Channels that communicate messages*
Key decision-makers and influencers: _____
Key business objectives and desired impacts: _____
Key customer conversation touch-points we need to impact: _____

Solution Messaging Process: *Cross-functional messaging process*
Key solutions groups or business units we need to coordinate: _____
Ideal cross-functional CMM leader in our organization: _____
Ultimate decision-making authority for solutions content: _____

Sales Performance Audit: *Depth of messaging to tell the story*
Unique messages to support specific conversations or sales teams: _____
Sales competency or performance issues: _____
Key opportunities to provide deeper sales cycle support: _____

Key Chapter Take-Aways

- **The CMM Message Map is deceptively simple**. It's easily communicated, practical, and manageable. We believe that the process must be simple—because the problem we are tackling, customer messaging, is not.
- Companies choose various CMM targets **depending on where they need to support sales in generating revenue**. Some focus on customer retention; others on new customer acquisition; others on building sales competency with specific decision-makers or in specific markets; others to combine solutions or expand offerings after a merger/acquisition.
- **Practical market segmentation and targeted decision-maker confirmation is key** to driving the scope and next steps of your Customer Message Management project. Targeted, segmented,

customer-focused messaging is a foundational premise and helps you prioritize and phase-in the content development.

- **Mapping the messaging requirements to the sales process** is rarely done in organizations today. This single exercise can bring clarity to both sales and marketing, and define how you will implement our Message Map.

In the next chapter we will apply the Message Map to our first practical step in developing your customer messaging—the *Cross-Functional Messaging Workshop.*

CHAPTER 8

CROSS-FUNCTIONAL MESSAGING WORKSHOP

In the last chapter we covered the critical decisions that your company will make as you build a CMM Message Map—specifically, which market segments, customer conversations, and sales resources will help the company drive revenue and meet key sales goals.

Now we're ready for a cross-functional CMM Messaging Workshop. The process that we will use has been implemented by over 150 companies—large global corporations, service companies in various industries, highly technical organizations, and small start-up businesses.

As you prepare for the workshop, it's important that you select a manageable—but meaningful—target. This target should be clear and understandable to the company and to everyone who participates in the workshop. Consider this statement:

"For the _____ market or segment, our _____ sales channel engages in sales conversations with _____ customers to position and sell _____ solutions."

Some examples:

- "For the health-care industry, our direct salespeople have conversations with CFOs, Health Information Directors, and physicians to sell our complete line of technology and services."
- "For the underground utility sub-segment of the heavy construction market, our dealers have conversations with construction company owners and fleet managers to sell or lease appropriate equipment, services, and support."
- "For the food manufacturing industry, our Web site initiates sales conversations with process engineers, compliance directors, and maintenance supervisors to create awareness and interest in our various automation components."
- "For existing customers who have been on a maintenance agreement for more than five years, our telesales team talks to purchasing and office managers to renew their agreements and identify equipment upgrade opportunities."

The people who participate in the workshop will be those who understand the target segment, the decision-makers and their business needs, and the positioning of your solutions specific to those needs. In other words, we'll need to assemble a group of "A" players who know how to have successful conversations with the target audience, which we want to capture and then replicate for the rest of the company.

Structure of the Messaging Workshop

The Messaging Workshop is typically a one- to two-day exercise with cross-functional resources (sales, services, and marketing) to develop the conversational content for six to eight customer needs. The workshop requires a facilitator who understands the CMM process and can keep the group focused on the desired results. It also requires a writer who listens with a customer-tuned ear and is able to distill the workshop input to the essential components of the Message Map. We'll talk more about writer attributes and writing style in Chapter 9.

Specifically, the purpose of the workshop is to populate "Conversation Roadmaps™" (Figure 8-1) by working with the people who best communicate to your target industry or buyer type. This means agreeing on the business needs that they hear repeatedly from customers, mapping your capabilities and solutions to those needs, determining the value of your solution as it solves each need, and identifying the proof points that justify your story.

The workshop is conducted as an interactive session led by a facilitator who can guide the group through the messaging process and keep everyone on task. The participant's job is to be open, conversant, and ready to work collaboratively to develop the messages that can inform your promotions, customer collaterals, and sales-ready support.

The power of the workshop comes in gaining joint buy-in from key opinion leaders regarding the types of conversations and supporting messaging needed to support the desired consultative, solutions-selling approach. The session is hard work, and very rewarding. In fact, many times the participants leave the workshop asking for a copy of the raw content—because it represents the best thinking of your company in terms of the conversations they want to consistently and repeatedly have with customers, starting with their business needs and working through your best-answer solution.

Below are the components of CMM messaging on a one-page CMM Conversation Roadmap. And yes, you can achieve this content in the Messaging Workshop! We have used this process repeatedly with consistent

Figure 8-1

CMM Conversation Roadmap

Target Audience: Name of the targeted conversation (decision-maker in what market segment?)
Business Need: What is the person trying to accomplish?
• Probing Questions—guided discussion to determine if this is a real problem, need, or goal?
• Related Business Pains—what are the challenges that are keeping them from meeting the need?
• Compelling Industry Statistics—relevant 3rd party data to focus the need discussion toward your solution.
• Potential Business Impact—what is the business upside of successfully achieving this goal or fixing the problem?

Solution Mapping	Diagnostic Questions	Potential Solution Scenario	Contextual Value Creation
Capability #1 Name	Specific questions designed to determine the potential need and impact of this capability.	Describe this capability as it can be applied or "used" by the customer to help meet the business goal.	Describe the relevant value that can be created if this capability is used in such a way—quantitative if possible.
Capability #2 Name			
Capability #3 Name			

Solution Value Summary Statement: Summarize the overall value and impact of these capabilities as applied to achieving this goal.

Supporting Proof Points: Competitive differentiation and 3rd-party validation.

results. More importantly, experience shows that this core content is exactly what is needed to inform the various documents and conversations that your sales channels want to have with customers.

Who to Invite   The primary participants are your "A players" for the target industry, segment, or solution. Think of this dream team as the ideal set of three to five people that you would choose to have on a sales call for the selected industry, segment, or solution.

Other attendees may include sales training, sales management, product management, marketing communications, other integrated marketing functions, and others who want to observe and learn.

Room Logistics   If possible, we suggest that you set up the room so that the salespeople and other core participants are seated in a horseshoe. This helps the facilitator keep them focused and engaged.

We also recommend that you provide additional tables and chairs at the back of the room for those who want to observe, or who may be in and out of the room during the workshop. This helps minimize distractions.

Additional requirements include a PC projector, two flipcharts, several pads of Post-It Notes, masking tape, and markers (see Figure 8-2).

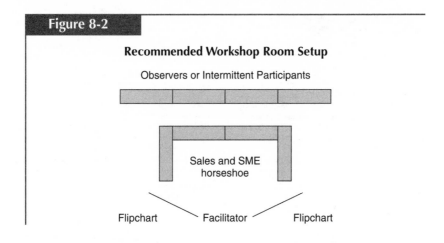

Figure 8-2

Recommended Workshop Room Setup

Observers or Intermittent Participants

Sales and SME
horseshoe

Flipchart   Facilitator   Flipchart

Sample Email to Participants   "Thanks for talking with me about the importance of the customer messaging project. We're at a critical point where we need input from you and others on the sales team. We would like you to participate in a 'Customer Messaging Workshop' on [dates]. The workshop will follow a proven process for identifying the conversations that you have—repeatedly and successfully—with your customers. There will be approximately five other salespeople in the workshop with you. The agenda and travel details are attached.

"You were selected specifically because the company would like to map our messages to the way that you and other successful salespeople identify customer needs, position our solutions, and present business value. Duplicating your success is important as we transition from product-focused marketing to customer-needs-focused messages.

"While there's no preparation necessary, we've attached a few questions to think about as you travel to the workshop, based on the input that you and other salespeople gave us in the phone interviews. Thank you!"

Sample Workshop Agenda   The workshop agenda typically looks like this:

Approximate Timing	Workshop Activity
15–30 minutes	**Management introduction** to describe the project goal and the importance of the group's participation
30 minutes–1 hour	**CMM introduction**—what CMM is, why it makes sense for the company, the messaging segment or target, and the process for today's work

1 hour	**Step 1: Key conversation list**—to confirm the decision-makers and influencers who play a role in the sale—from your Message Map
2 hours	**Step 2: Opportunity development**—to develop and confirm the key customer business needs, goals, or problems, and associated challenges or pain points
1–1.5 hour *per business need*	**Steps 3 & 4: Solution mapping and value creation**—to identify key corresponding capabilities, diagnostic questions, application scenarios, and value statements related to solving each of the confirmed business needs
1 hour	**Step 5: Proof points combined with message implementation**—to identify how and when sales would use this messaging to move sales cycles forward to close, and where more depth or proof points are required
15–30 minutes	**Summary and next steps**

The Workshop Process

It's important that the marketing team—and specifically the workshop facilitator—understand the workshop process, goals, and tools for driving out the conversational content. As an overview, there are fundamentally two activities that you will complete in the workshop, as shown in Figure 8-3:

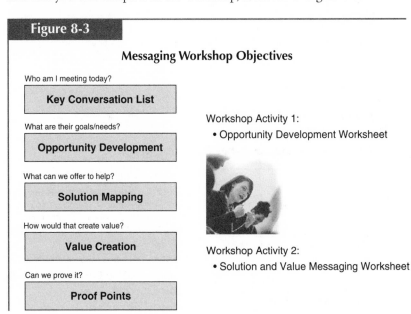

Figure 8-3

Messaging Workshop Objectives

Who am I meeting today?

Key Conversation List

What are their goals/needs?

Opportunity Development

What can we offer to help?

Solution Mapping

How would that create value?

Value Creation

Can we prove it?

Proof Points

Workshop Activity 1:
• Opportunity Development Worksheet

Workshop Activity 2:
• Solution and Value Messaging Worksheet

Workshop Activity 1: Opportunity Development Worksheet

The purpose of this activity is "opportunity development"—defining who your salespeople talk to as part of the sale (buyer roles), and the business issues that those customers are trying to address (buyer goals).

Workshop Activity 2: Solution and Value Messaging Worksheet

The purpose of this activity is "solution development"—mapping the specific capabilities that solve each buyer goal, identifying the business value of solving the problem with those capabilities, and developing the proof points that validate your value claim.

We'll walk through each step in the process and provide a content example.

Step 1: Buyer Roles—Who am I meeting with today?

Goal—Identify the types of buyers who are regularly and purposely involved in the sale. (Figure 8-4)

- What is their role in the sale and final decision?
- Can you categorize the buyer roles? For example, coach, user, financial buyer, executive buyer. Or influencer versus decision-maker.
- In general, what is the profile of each buyer: business hot buttons, personal wins, buying style, or preferences?

Facilitation Notes:

- It helps to first establish the sales-process steps, and then discuss the types of buyers in terms of when and why they are involved in the decision.

Figure 8-4

Example—Key Conversation List

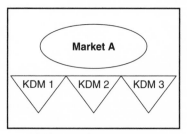

KDM = Key Decision Maker

Sample company: CMM Group

CMM Group offers Customer Message Management services to companies who want to improve sales and marketing effectiveness through integration of the two functions.

Market A: Sales and Marketing Effectiveness

KDM 1: CMO/VP Marketing

KDM 2: CSO/VP Sales

KDM 3: Director Sales Training

- Keep the workshop group focused on the key conversations that move the sale forward—not every person that they could possibly talk to in an account.
- Find a way to categorize the buyer roles in some way. For example, if your reps sell to multiple job titles in marketing—VP Marketing, Catalog Marketing, Internet Marketing, Marketing Manager, etc.—determine if the general conversations with "marketing" are the same, or if the buyer goals are truly different among the different marketing types. As the facilitator, your job is to simplify, not complicate!

Step 2: Buyer Goals—What are their goals/needs?

Goal—Identify the customer's goals or needs—what they are trying to accomplish or solve? (Figure 8-5)

- What are the needs, problems, or requirements of decision-makers in this industry/segment? List each goal (I need to . . .) and briefly describe it from the customer's perspective.
- For each business need, what challenges or "pain points" do decision-makers face in trying to achieve the goal? List three or four challenges per business need.
- What is the potential business impact if the business need is or is not addressed? What is gained and/or saved?

Figure 8-5

Example—Business Needs and Challenges

KDM 1: CMO/VP Marketing
Business Issues
☐ BI 1: Create "one voice" across customer touchpoints
☐ BI 2: Elevate from product to problem marketing
☐ **BI 3: Build marketing collateral that salespeople will use**

Challenges related to BI 3:
- Sales creates maverick messages and tools, and we lose brand consistency
- Current value propositions are too lofty and not differentiated enough to support compelling customer conversations
- Current collaterals are focused on what we sell—products, features, and technical functions—not what customers want to do

BI = Business Issue

Facilitation Notes:

- While you can prepare for this step using industry research or persona profiles from marketing, you need to identify the real-world customer goals that your best salespeople hear every day. It's important to understand these "key conversations" from a feet-in-the-street perspective.
- Consider using a *Sticky Note Exercise* for this step. Give each salesperson a packet of sticky notes, such as 3M Post-It Notes, and ask them to write one business goal on each note for a given buyer role. Collect the notes and consolidate the various business goals to develop a "short list." Work with the group to restate each business goal on the short list in customer terms, and prioritize them based on what is most important to the customer.
- This step typically results in six to eight unique buyer goals per decision-maker—and fewer (three or four) for executive buyers. If the number of goals is becoming unwieldy, we suggest using a rating system to prioritize the goals. For example, you might plot "importance to customer" versus "our ability to solve this problem" to determine the business goals that fall within your company's "sweet spot."
- For each of the confirmed buyer goals, you should identify at least three pain points, challenges, or obstacles to achieving those goals. This is a critical step because it will serve to guide you in the next step of choosing which capabilities (products, services, programs) can be applied to create a solution. (Figure 8-6)

Step 3: Solution Map—What can we offer to help?

Goal—Map your company's best-answer capabilities—products, services, programs, features—that uniquely and specifically address each business goal.

- List the three to five best-answer capabilities that make up the solution and specifically address the business need. Use your pain point/ challenge list under each goal or need as a guide for identifying the most relevant capabilities. Avoid applying everything; select the capabilities that are most relevant.
- Diagnostic Questions: For each capability or for the solution, identify one to three questions that probe for the potential need and impact as it addresses the need.
- Potential Solution Scenario: For each capability, write a "What if you could . . . " question that shows the customer how they would use it to solve the problem.

Figure 8-6

Example—Opportunity Development Worksheet	
Business Issue—We need to build marketing collateral and salespeople will use (ROI)	
Description	**Related Pain Points / Challenges**
Statistics indicate that up to 90% of the content created for sales support goes unused in the field, and that over 97% of campaigns are irrelevant to the customers they were intended to attract. Further, salespeople spend 40–60 hours per month creating messaging and customizing collaterals for use with customers. In a highly competitive marketplace, this is one place where a small change could make a big difference.	• Sales creates maverick messages and tools, and we lose brand consistency • Current value propositions are too lofty and not differentiated enough to support compelling customer conversations • Current collaterals are focused on what we sell—products, features, and technical functions—not what customers want to do

Probing Questions
- What is the "best practices" sales process used by your sales team today? Are the steps of that process reflected in your CRM or opportunity management system? Is marketing taught the same methodology?
- Where does sales seem to be having the biggest hurdles in terms of moving opportunities through the funnel—in creating leads, cultivating sales, closing and differentiating your solutions, or retaining customers and cross-selling?
- What stages of the sales cycle do most of your collaterals support? Ideally, how would you like to see your messages and collaterals used throughout the sales process?
- What feedback does your sales team provide on your messages and marketing collaterals? How do you measure return on marketing investment?

Compelling Fact
According to a B2B online survey, 70% of marketers graded themselves as failing to support critical customer conversations in a way that helps salespeople sell solutions or value.

Potential Business Impact
Marketing materials that support the critical "moments of truth" in the customer buying process are more likely to be used by sales because they reinforce a solution-selling dialogue with customers—making marketing more relevant to revenue-generating activities.

Facilitation Notes:

- You may need to adjust the Conversation Roadmap to reflect your company's sales training methodology. For example, Huthwaite SPIN Selling, Customer-Centric Selling, and others prescribe specific questioning sequences, tools, and techniques.
- Use the "challenges or pain points" as hints or clues for the kinds of capabilities and questions that should be applied in a customer conversation.

- This activity works best when your sales reps speak to you the same way they would speak to a customer, as if they were role-playing the customer conversation. Keep reminding them that you want to hear how they talk to the customer—and that they don't have to worry about "wordsmithing" or choosing their words carefully. That's your job!
- More is not better! In today's selling environment, playing "20 questions" with customers is less productive than asking a few excellent questions that hone in on the real issue. As your sales reps talk, listen for the progression of the conversation—what they ask to set up the situation, how they dig deeper to reveal the customer's "pain points," and ultimately how they position your capability (via the Possible Solution Scenario).

Step 4: Value Creation—How does that "solution" create value?

Goal—Identify the measurable value that results when a customer solves their business problem or goal with your solution (capabilities). (Figure 8-7)

- Capability value and differentiation: Describe the value each capability provides specifically in response to this business need.
- Solution value summary and differentiation: Describe the value that this solution provides specifically in response to this business need.

Facilitation Notes:

- Push the sales team to tell you what the customer really cares about in terms of results. For example, what the company promotes as a "benefit" might not be meaningful to the customer, in the context of solving the business problem.
- Seek measurable value (%, $, ±).
- It sometimes helps for sales reps to think of value in terms of past customer successes—the results that other customers have seen by implementing the capabilities or solution. If they take this route, make sure that the business problem that was solved in the success story is the same as the customer goal that you are discussing.

Step 5: Proof Points—Can you prove that your solution can create value?

Goal—Identify the best proof points—customer successes, third-party validation, research data—that substantiate your value claim. (Figure 8-8)

- What proof points demonstrate our ability to provide the stated value?

Figure 8-7

Sample Solution and Value Messaging Worksheet			
Business Issue—We need to build marketing collateral that salespeople will use (ROI)			
Capability	**Diagnostic Questions**	**Solution Scenario**	**Value Creation Statement**
Sales-cycle-relevant deliverable design	• Which collaterals are used most often by sales? Why? • How closely synchronized are your collaterals with the steps of the sales process? • At what stage of the sales process do salespeople struggle most in communicating your solutions and value to customers? How could marketing help?	What if marketing could use a simple process for mapping sales support and customer collaterals to the rhythm of the sales cycle, reinforcing the "best practices" sales process in support of revenue generation?	CMM Group's Deliverable Design Workshop identifies the steps of the customer buying process, determines the key "moments of truth" in selling, and creates an anatomy for each document, so that marketing can build a "selling toolkit" that reinforces the sales cycle. • Increase the relevance of marketing to the sales process • Eliminate un-used or irrelevant collaterals (and associated costs) • Reduce marketing time by using templates for deliverables that use the Conversation Roadmap content
Conversational messaging			
Conversational Competency training			

- What types of proofs work best at the point of sale to build credibility in our solution?

Facilitation Notes:

- While salespeople generally crave good proof points, they may not know what information exists; they may need to rely on you to find the best proof points.
- Sometimes this step is done after the workshop, with the marketing team. If this is the course that you take, be sure to ask the sales reps what types of proof points would be most meaningful to the customer who is making a buying decision about your company.

Figure 8-8

Sample Solution Summary and Proof Points

Business Issue—We need to build marketing collateral that salespeople will use (ROI)

Solution summary
CMM Group helps you create messages and marketing communications that reinforce your sales process and align with the way customers want to consume information in the decision-making process. By supporting the sales process and working with sales management to identify where messaging can impact the time from lead to close, marketing can gain more relevance to revenue generation.

Proof point
CMM companies outdistance others in quota achievement by 25%, with win rates that are 20% higher than for the general population of sales forces.
Source: CSO Insights, "Sales Effectiveness Insights: Optimizing Sales Performance with Consistent Message Management, 2004"

Success story
"We reduced our marketing communications budget by $350,000 in the first six months by identifying and eliminating the collaterals that did not reinforce the sales process."
Source: CMM Group Customer, 2004

"One of our salespeople had never talked to a CFO in his life. He cold-called a CFO in an account using the new messaging and sales tools. He got an appointment for the next day, used the CMM tools and messages in the meeting, defined the CFO's goals, and got the guy so excited about what we could do that he called all of his lower-level decision-makers into his office while the salesperson was still there. Our rep left the meeting with a clear plan for closure. That tells me the messaging is working."
Source: CMM Group Customer, 2005

Does it Have to be a Workshop?

Sometimes it might not be practical or feasible to gather your "A" reps in a room together for the Messaging Workshop. For example, people from global regions or busy travelers sometimes cannot be present on the big day. In some cases we've successfully conducted a series of shorter workshops or phone calls to include important participants.

Another option is to work with a cross-functional team to develop the key conversation list (who am I talking to and what do they care about?), and then divide the resulting business needs among sub-teams for content development. We can often move quickly in sub-teams, because we are focused on a single business need; however, we strongly recommend a validation workshop with the "dream team" at some point to confirm that the primary messages are agreed upon by all.

Here are recommendations for using an alternate workshop method:

- Call them Messaging Workshops—even if it's more of a roundtable or a phone call.
- Do a CMM overview with the whole team via webcast, conference call, or in person prior to the workshops so that everyone understands the process and Message Map.
- Kick off each session with a quick review of the Message Map and process.
- Keep good control over the process, so that a "roundtable" doesn't become too informal or lose site of the end goals.
- Use flipcharts and whiteboards, even in a small-group setting; or a webcast if online, so that participants can immediately see their input entered into the CMM templates.
- Validate the messages with the whole "dream team" before launch.

Key Chapter Take-Aways

- Select a **manageable—but meaningful—messaging project** for the workshop, such as an industry, a particular type of decision-maker, or a specific solution. The project focus should be easily understood by everyone who participates in the workshop.
- Involve a **cross-functional team** consisting of your "A" players—the people who best communicate the message to customers. The goal is not the number of people in the workshop—more people is not always better. The goal is to involve the people who repeatedly and successfully tell the story.
- The **best-practices** Messaging Workshop is conducted as a concentrated 1.5 to 2.0-day session; however, if not practical to involve all participants in the workshop, consider using phone workshops or web-based workshops as an alternative.
- When developing a **key conversation list,** remember that identifying the buyer types helps you categorize business needs; and identify the critical buyers that salespeople need to involve when building a business case.
- In the **solution mapping** step, avoid solving every business need with every capability or solution that you sell; conversely, avoid being non-specific or too "high level" in your mapping. The capabilities that

solve each business need should be directly applicable to that need, and should be stated in the right terms and level of depth for the given buyer type.

- In the **value creation** step, focus on measurable value as much as possible. If you're developing value statements for executives, then focus on the metrics that they use to evaluate and manage company performance.

CHAPTER 9

MESSAGE DEVELOPMENT AND VALIDATION

The Cross-Functional Messaging Workshop represents a snapshot in time. You will spend two days draining the brains of some of the brightest folks in the company; however, recognize that not everyone you need in the room will make it to the workshop, nor are the participants immediately able to grasp everything they need to provide "in the moment." In those cases, you may want to spend extra time in post-workshop message development and validation to gather their valuable input.

This next step is turning these raw outputs from the workshop into messaging that you can use for sales coaching and customer-facing content. This step is called *message development and validation.* In this chapter we will provide exercises for creating CMM content and best-practice examples of completed worksheets to give you a benchmark for building content that will stand up in the field and in front of customers.

- **Message development.** The CMM Conversation Roadmap™, introduced in Chapter 8, guides the creation of all the necessary messaging components needed to help salespeople conduct a consultative conversation and equip them with supporting communications tools. We've turned the worksheet into a copywriting template that can be used to guide the message creation process.
- **Content validation.** Validation is critical to the CMM process. Making sure the messaging is useful in the field and in front of customers is part of this step in the project. We will describe a recommended approach for reviewing, validating, and updating content with salespeople and your target audience.

Message Development

The Customer Message Management approach focuses on process—creating messaging from the outside-in based on customer roles and goals. It's important to note, however, that just having the right "boxes" and "connection points" in place doesn't mean you'll get good content.

Customer Message Management also requires awareness and sensitivity to the tone and manner with which you craft your messaging. To help you out, we've put together a simple quiz and T.I.P.S. sheet. The point is not to test your copywriting skills, but to provide a reminder of what you should be trying to accomplish:

- **We connect with customers when they find our messages are:**

    A. All about us—our company, products, and services
    B. Broad, far-reaching, and all-encompassing
    C. Relevant to their situation
    D. Complex, jargon-laced, and aggressive

The answer, of course, is "C." Given that we are bombarded with more information in one day than our ancestors received in a year, messaging must be focused on customer needs and challenges in order to make an impression. Targeted messages are just that—sharp, to the point, and designed to break through the clutter. If your audience sees that your messages are less about you and more about them, then you've made a connection that will set you apart from others vying for their attention.

- **Our customer messaging should be:**

    A. Informational
    B. Responsive to customer needs
    C. Corporate and impersonal
    D. Promotional exaggeration

It's a trick question. The correct answer is "B," followed by "A." You need to demonstrate real empathy for what customers are trying to accomplish and then give them the information—not puffery—that will help them arrive at a solution. While this may seem obvious, review some of your collateral, presentations, and other marketing materials and see how well they score.

Understanding the principles behind good copy is one thing. How do you actually write copy that is relevant, responsive, and informational? Well, it's not rocket science … and you don't need to be a professional copywriter. But it does require the ability to listen with a customer-tuned ear.

There are four basic tenets—we call them T.I.P.S.—to crafting customer-relevant copy. If you follow these suggestions, your content will become more clear, compelling, and persuasive. It can help you turn prospects into customers, and customers into long-term relationships. (You might want to clip this reminder.)

Figure 9-1

CMM—Content Creation T.I.P.S.

- **T**alk to customers in *their* language; be relevant and show respect for the customer's situation; don't preach from your product-centric viewpoint.
- **I**dentify with the challenges your customers face; demonstrate an *empathy* for your customer's business, and an accurate assessment of your potential impact.
- **P**osition your company's products and services in terms of how they can *respond* to customer's needs or solve their problems.
- **S**how how your company's products and services can help a customer *achieve* desired value in the customer's context.

How do you put T.I.P.S. into action? Sometimes the best way to communicate a concept is by showing before-and-after examples. Here are some samples of how your customer messaging content can be improved using the CMM T.I.P.S. approach:

Talk with customers, not at them—Don't be afraid to sound personal. Customers tune out most marketing messages because they don't feel the content is relevant to them. Be willing to use "you" in your copy. Write in the first person, "I" or "we." And write in a familiar, informal tone that uses the cadence or rhythms of natural spoken language. Don't preach or be overly official if you don't have to. (See Figure 9-2.)

Figure 9-2

Example—Talk with Customers

Before	After
"Employee retention issues can have a significant negative impact on company productivity and operating costs."	"Dealing with employee turnover can slow down your business and cost you money."

Identify with the problems they face—It's about them, not you. You are not the center of their universe, so your messages shouldn't sound like you are. Engage customers with real, relevant issues they care about and that impact their business. Position the message in terms of their needs—and avoid using marketing-speak that is too promotional, such as corporate acronyms or internal terminology that the customer may not be familiar with. (See Figure 9-3.)

Figure 9-3

Example—Identify with the Problem

Before	After
"Our best-in-class Stratus 1000 Job Preview Solution and S.T.I.C Compensation Programs will keep your business growing and moving forward." "By ensuring all of our placements have passed a realistic job preview prior to coming on board, as well as offering the industry's leading compensation package, we ensure you will have the staffing engine needed to keep your business running."	"If you struggle keeping temporary staff on the job, it may have a negative impact on the ability of your line managers and supervisors to meet their business goals." "That's why we only provide staffing talent that has demonstrated interest and commitment to your assignment. And we add incentive compensation to make sure they finish your job."

Position based on what they want to accomplish—Engage customers by starting a dialogue about an aspect of their business, not just your offering. Share a statistic or insight about the topic, so they want to learn more. Use thought-provoking statements and open-ended questions. Be very careful, though, when trying to use clever humor. (See Figure 9-4.)

Figure 9-4

Example—Position Based on Their Goals

Before	After
"Not knowing if your temporary workers are going to stay or go can really put you between a rock and a hard placement." "Ask about our industry-leading StayPut™ Promise. We're the only staffing firm willing to guarantee that our placements will meet your needs and stay the course." "That's why more companies choose us for their administrative staffing requirements."	"What would it cost you if 70 percent of your temporary staff needed to be replaced before their assignments ended?" "That's the average turnover for most staffing firms. But you can't afford to be average when it comes to managing costs—so we won't let you." "You'll get real business benefits from our 98 percent satisfaction and job completion rating, such as avoiding unplanned and unwanted turnover costs."

Show them how you can help achieve value—Customers control their businesses, you don't. It's up to them to determine how important you are to their lives. Offer them solutions that can help their business. Frame these solutions as questions that allow the person to consider the impact or potential value. Don't make it sound like you have all the answers or make the customer feel like they have no choice. (See Figure 9-5.)

Figure 9-5

Example—Show the Value

Before	After
"Don't be caught short. We offer a powerful way to make sure your temporary help stays for the long haul." "Sign up now for our Straus 1,000 employee screening and qualification system and give your business the productivity boost it desperately needs."	"What if you knew your temporary staff had already previewed, performed, and stated a preference for your assignment—prior to even showing up?" "How much would this increase your confidence that a temp will jump in and quickly become a valued contributor?"

Even though it's not officially part of the CMM T.I.P.S. chart, it should go without saying that you should always *be brief.* Customers are busy people. Respecting their time is one way to show you understand their needs. Get to the point and let them know what to do next. Keep the message as simple and clear as possible. Avoid giving unnecessary details or promoting topics that aren't relevant to the situation. (See Figure 9-6.)

What Makes Good CMM Writing Great

Cut the BS—the Beautiful Style. Pretty sentences don't translate to good messaging. Marketing jargon—a language unto itself that favors words like optimize, minimize, and other low-information words, non-specific points, and empty phrases—doesn't do it.

We experienced the following situation in a Messaging Workshop: The facilitator was helping the group work on a value statement, and a top sales rep said, "The value is that they eliminate the quality control step, which cuts 3–10 days out of the process. Every day adds more cost and frustration. We have several case studies showing how we've helped customers save budget over the life of the project."

Figure 9-6

Keep It Brief

Before	After
"Ensure your temporary staff has been screened, qualified, and tested to determine whether they are the right job fit. Regardless of your own HR resource and skill levels, we can ensure that this important part of the staffing process is managed more effectively. In addition, we've created a compensation program that includes extra incentives to encourage our placements to complete the job, including some of the industry's most lucrative bonus programs. All of this, to help reduce your concerns over temporary staffing turnover and production."	"You can get pre-tested, temporary employees who demonstrate the skills and desire needed to do your job right. In addition, we take the responsibility off your shoulders to make sure they stay on the job as long as you need them."

The writer wrote "minimizes resources."

The bottom line is that meaningful, memorable, well-reasoned writing that concisely emphasizes points that the customer cares about results in good messaging.

- Words to avoid: efficiency and effectiveness, optimize, minimize, maximize, high quality, create value, improved, and other vacuous phrases.
- If you can't explain what you just wrote, the odds are no one else will be able to either.
- Don't fill content boxes for the sake of filling boxes with content. If you feel like you're "making it up" or writing "fluff," then go back to your sales team to clarify the point.
- Always relate your content blocks back to the customer's business need—the reason for the "story" that you are telling.
- Make value points tangible, measurable, and practical, as much as possible. If you can't credibly state the value to a customer with a straight face, then the sales team won't say it either.
- Read the whole Conversation Roadmap, start to finish, before you declare the draft "done." Does it stay focused on the business need? Does it follow a consultative selling flow—business problem, challenges, solution, value, proof? Is it a convincing conversation?
- Use your "who cares" measuring stick continuously as you write.

CMM Conversation Roadmap™

Now that we've established writing tone and manner, let's look at the CMM message development template—the Conversation Roadmap. The purpose of this template is to provide a repeatable structure for creating customer-focused, sales-ready messaging. It identifies specific copy elements that fuel a consultative selling dialogue.

One copy of the Conversation Roadmap is populated for each business need—for a given decision-maker and market segment. So, for example, if you have confirmed ten key business needs for a COO decision-maker in the manufacturing sector, you will be completing ten Conversation Roadmaps.

The completed template becomes your "core content." It is the document you will use to ultimately inform and populate the various tools needed along a sales cycle. Given that end goal, the copy blocks have been carefully identified, organized, and described based on the ultimate end-uses for the messaging inside sales coaching or customer-facing outputs.

Earlier we showed you a one-page version of the Conversation Roadmap. It helps to keep all of the required messaging in one place. From here, you can envision the "story" that needs to be created. This is the opposite of event-driven messaging: creating the presentation . . . the sell sheet . . . the "this" and the "that." Without a comprehensive approach, the story never comes together.

Imagine if your response to a customer business need was consistent from the prospect's first Web site experience through the sales conversation, presentation, and proposal. This becomes more possible when you treat the story or answer to that customer business need as a strategic corporate asset first, and then parse that story into its appropriate deliverables.

The key is that this process is "guided" by a consistent, repeatable structure that can be adopted and used throughout the company. We propose the Conversation Roadmap as the necessary structure for this typically unstructured process.

Now let's take a detailed look at this tool, and describe the actual messaging components you will need to create.

The Opportunity Development Worksheet portion is designed to ensure we capture the complete essence of the customer business need. It's not just a bullet point on a slide; it's a real-life opportunity to solve pains, challenges, and help achieve a strategic business objective. (See Figure 9-7.)

The Opportunity Development Workshop includes five copy boxes:

1. **Business Need Description.** Name the business need and describe the reason customers are struggling and trying to solve this problem.

Figure 9-7

Example—Opportunity Development Worksheet

Business Issue—We need to build marketing collateral and salespeople will use (ROI)	
Description	**Related Pain Points / Challenges**
Statistics indicate that up to 90% of the content created for sales support goes unused in the field, and that over 97% of campaigns are irrelevant to the customers they were intended to attract. Further, salespeople spend 40–60 hours per month creating messaging and customizing collaterals for use with customers. In a highly competitive marketplace, this is one place where a small change could make a big difference.	• Sales creates maverick messages and tools, and we lose brand consistency • Current value propositions are too lofty and not differentiated enough to support compelling customer conversations • Current collaterals are focused on what we sell—products, features, and technical functions—not what customers want to do

Probing Questions
- What is the "best practices" sales process used by your sales team today? Are the steps of that process reflected in your CRM or opportunity management system? Is marketing taught the same methodology?
- Where does sales seem to be having the biggest hurdles in terms of moving opportunities through the funnel—in creating leads, cultivating sales, closing and differentiating your solutions, or retaining customers and cross-selling?
- What stages of the sales cycle do most of your collaterals support? Ideally, how would you like to see your messages and collaterals used throughout the sales process?
- What feedback does your sales team provide on your messages and marketing collaterals? How do you measure return on marketing investment?

Compelling Fact
According to a B2B online survey, 70% of marketers graded themselves as failing to support critical customer conversations in a way that helps salespeople sell solutions or value.

Potential Business Impact
Marketing materials that support the critical "moments of truth" in the customer buying process are more likely to be used by sales because they reinforce a solution-selling dialogue with customers—making marketing more relevant to revenue-generating activities.

2. **Probing Questions.** Draft a series of questions that can be asked or considered by the customer to help determine or confirm if the business need is relevant to their current business situation.

3. **Related Pain Points/Challenges.** Identify a list of business challenges that are currently keeping companies from addressing the business need; demonstrate your awareness and knowledge of the pains customers are struggling with.

4. **Compelling Fact.** Identify compelling industry statistics, trends, or other current data that reinforce the realities of and risks associated with not effectively dealing with this business need.

5. **Potential Business Impact.** Describe the potential upside of successfully overcoming the challenges, eliminating the pains, and meeting the business need.

Below is a sample Opportunity Development Worksheet (Figure 9-8) that would result from the Messaging Workshop. We have completed the business issue description, related pain points, probing questions and a compelling fact.

Figure 9-8

Opportunity Development Worksheet

Business Issue—We need to reduce turnover of temporary staff	
Description	**Related Pain Points / Challenges**
Finding the right temporary, administrative support can be a challenge.	• Getting temporaries that are not a good fit with the assignment or the culture
At first glance, this may appear to be a simple position to fill, but experience tells you there's a potential for huge headaches and frustration if you don't do it right.	• Temporary staff doesn't have a broad enough skill set to flex with the job requirements
On the other hand, when you find the right help, it makes all the difference in the world in terms of departmental productivity, employee satisfaction, and overall smooth business operation. So, what does it take to do it right?	• Temporaries are too easily lured away before finishing the job

Probing Questions
- Are you struggling with temporary administrative staff who are unreliable, unhappy with their assignments, a poor cultural fit, or who leave too quickly for better job offers?
- How does frequent turnover of temporary staff impact your company, in terms of training and re-training time? Customer continuity? Morale of other employees?
- What is your best method for recruiting temp employees? Are you usually hiring to fill a temporary position, or hoping to find someone who will fit the job and culture as a long-term employee?

Compelling Fact
It costs up to 30% of a position's first-year salary to replace and re-train after turnover—not including the time, frustration, and potential demotivation of other employees who are affected by the turnover.

Potential Business Impact
Reducing turnover impacts staffing costs, minimizes training time, and improves morale of other employees who work with the temporary employee on a daily basis and want consistency of workflow, as well as dependable co-workers.

Figure 9-9

Sample Opportunity Development
Worksheet—SPIN Selling

Business Issue—We need to reduce turnover of temporary staff

Provide questions that follow your sales team's preferred sales
methodology:

Situation Questions
- What is your best method for recruiting temp employees? Are you
  usually hiring to fill a temporary position, or hoping to find someone
  who will fit the job and culture as a long-term employee?

Problem Questions
- Are you struggling with temporary administrative staff who are
  unreliable, unhappy with their assignments, a poor cultural fit, or who
  leave too quickly for better job offers?

Implication Questions
- How does frequent turnover of temporary staff impact your company,
  in terms of training and re-training time? Customer continuity? Morale
  of other employees?

Needs Payoff Questions
- How might it help turnover to have temporary staff employees who had
  a realistic review of the position and had participated in a "day on the
  job" simulation before arriving at your company for their assignment?

We continue this example (Figure 9-9) to show how the Probing Questions can be structured to support the company's adopted selling methodology—in this case it's Neal Rackham's SPIN® Selling approach.

The next step is to create solution and value messaging. For this we've created an integrated template that connects the solution mapping and contextual value creation steps.

The Solution and Value Messaging Worksheet (Figure 9-10), is designed to guide you through the messaging components required in consultative customer communications. It's not just jumping to the named feature and providing a generic benefit statement; it's about creating a conversational "talk track" that encourages customer interaction and cooperation in developing a solution.

The Solution and Value Messaging Worksheet includes six copy boxes:

1. **Relevant Capability.** Descriptive phrase telling what your
   capability does (not a specific product or brand name) as it
   contributes to helping meet the business need.

Figure 9-10

Solution and Value Messaging Worksheet

Business Issue—			
Relevant Capabilities	**Diagnostic Questions**	**Solution Scenario (What if . . . ?)**	**Contextual Values Statement**
Solution Value Statement			
Proof Point			

2. **Diagnostic Discussion.** A series of questions designed to help the salesperson and customer "rule in" or "rule out" whether a capability is a fit, as well as help establish the customer context for value.

3. **Possible Solution Scenario.** Often written as a "what if" statement to help guide the customer to envisioning themselves potentially using the capability to successfully overcome a challenge and contribute to solving the ultimate business need.

4. **Contextual Value Statement.** At this point you can write a branded value statement that names your capability and describes the value it can potentially contribute in the context of the business need and mapped capability.

5. **Solution Value Summary.** This represents a truly unique piece of copy. Based on the mapped capabilities and values, you can now write a statement that is truly a "sum of the parts." This will ultimately serve as your elevator response for this business need, but it can only be written after you have done the solution mapping and written the contextual value messages.

6. **Proof Point.** For each story, we've identified the need for a proof point. It's a third-party validation of the claims you've made in the solution mapping and contextual value messaging section. More than likely, this is a brief customer testimonial to the fact that you can deliver—and have delivered—as promised.

On the next page there is a completed Solution and Value Messaging Worksheet (Figure 9-11), based on the example used previously in this chapter.

Figure 9-11

Example—Solution and Value Messaging Worksheet

Business Issue—We need to reduce turnover of temporary staff

Capability	Diagnostic Questions	Solution Scenario	Value Creation Statement
Pre-screening and Assessment	• How often do you find that administrative or temporary employees do not have the proper skills for the position? • What impact does that have on supervisors who struggle with temps who are unhappy or unreliable?	What if you only received candidates that had passed a rigorous pre-screening process matching their skills and personality to the position?	MP Staffing's Pre-Screening and Testing process thoroughly assess and qualify the candidate that's the best fit for the job. Proper screening and testing has been shown to lower turnover by 4x in the first 90 days.
Realistic Job Review	• How do you set realistic expectations about the job—especially if the temp believes that the job was supposed to be different that it is? • What's the impact of misplaced people in terms of cost to train and cost to replace?	What if, when your administrative employees showed up for work on day one, they had already been exposed to position-specific work tasks; experienced day-in-the life scenarios; viewed relevant job videos; and toured your facility to shadow a similar position?	MP's Job Review approach gives candidates a full understanding of the job requirements and work environment prior to arriving at your offices. This candid description and discussion "filters in" the people who are prepared and eager for the job.
Free Training Programs	• If someone needs to increase their skill level to meet job expectations, what are their best options to meet your requirements? • What's the impact of less-than-desirable skill-sets on workflow or the morale of other employees?	What if, when your administrative staff needed to update or increase their skill, they had free access to thousands of the most popular and applicable job-related training programs?	MP's Training Center offers free on-the-job training so that temporary staff can continuously upgrade their skills in response to your changing needs.

The "Solution Summary" is a key part of this worksheet because it combines the relevant capabilities to create a solution that is specific to the business issue. In the example below (Figure 9-12), we emphasize how MP Staffing uses Pre-screening and Assessment, Realistic Job Review, and Free Training Programs to address the root causes of employee turnover. The proof point demonstrates that MP Staffing has successfully implemented this solution with other similar clients.

Once you've completed both of these worksheets for each business need, you've produced a CMM Conversation Roadmap. And you've created a library of messaging that becomes a strategic corporate asset, which previously existed nowhere in the company—or possibly only inside the minds of your top salespeople!

Message Validation

After the workshop and completion of the draft Conversation Roadmap, it's time to validate the stories for frontline use. There are two key groups to seek for validation:

1. Workshop participants (sales and marketing)
2. Prospects and customers

Workshop Participants   First, go back to the participants of the workshop, who have now been designated your Customer Message Advisory Task

---

Figure 9-12

Example—Solution Summary and Proof Points

Business Issue—We need to reduce turnover of temporary staff

Solution summary
MP Staffing assumes the burden of finding candidates with the right fit, commitment, and skill sets necessary to pick up and stick with the job. Any solution must address the root causes of administrative turnover with proactive, pre-emptive programming. At MP Staffing, we've put together a comprehensive approach to decreasing unwanted turnover among temporary staff.

Proof point
"MP Staffing reduced turnover from 75% to 5% in the call center at ABC Global."
Source: Elizabeth Jones, Director of Administrative and Support Services, ABC Global

Force. (Remember to sign them up for this follow-through activity at the time of the workshop.)

There are several approaches to reaching out to this busy audience. Decide which one will work best for you. The key is to gain enough participation to provide confidence in the messaging, and create enough support from key company opinion leaders when it comes time to launch and leverage the content in the field.

Recommended Option: Online Web Conference Review   Our most successful approach involves online web conferencing with conference call-in. We send the content in advance to the Task Force. They are asked to use the Track Changes tool in *Microsoft Word* and send back their initial feedback. One person is charged with assembling that feedback into a "version 2" roadmap document.

Then the members of the team are invited to an online web conference where we put the v2 document live on the web using desktop sharing and conduct an online review session. The session is facilitated, and attendee input is managed, discussed, and agreed upon during the call. Your best typist and content person should "drive" the online document activity, inserting the agreed-upon changes for everyone to see and validate in real time.

Typically this process takes one to three calls to complete a first round of copy reviews. Schedule the calls for no more than two-hour increments. To maintain momentum, schedule the calls a couple of days apart, seeking to complete the content review within the two weeks post-workshop.

One other, similar option is to skip the online web editing portion and conduct a basic conference call soliciting everyone's input. Similar discussions take place and content changes are debated, but instead of real-time editing and wordsmithing, the input is gathered and you go offline to finesse the changes. The changes are resubmitted to the Task Force as version 3 for final feedback and approval.

In either case, these activities may have to be repeated as often as necessary for the team to be satisfied that you have created the compelling customer messaging required in the field.

Prospect and Customer Validation   While field sales personnel and experienced marketers can often represent the customers' viewpoint, it is ideal if your Customer Message Management project includes a reasonable review with prospects and customers.

The question usually arises—how do I get that input? Well, we're sorry to report, we haven't come up with any magic formulas. The options typically require the usual effort to get one-on-one direct customer contact.

Start with the sales participants on your Advisory Task Force. We've had success, where these salespeople identify two potential customers who'd be willing to accept an email attachment with the content; review the content offline; and then walk through a one-hour phone conversation with someone from your team to review their thoughts and provide feedback. For this effort, consider offering a token of appreciation—maybe a dinner gift certificate, golf card, or something that is appropriate given the current "gifting" constraints.

In other cases, we have put the messaging into a more formal "customer-facing" document and brought the content to trade shows to share in previously scheduled executive appointments. Honestly, we've had some clients go as far as to begin leveraging the new content into upcoming presentations and proposals to test response. The feeling is that the new messaging, while not fully validated with customers, is already better than the previous messaging, so that there's nothing to lose by "piloting" the content in real-world scenarios.

Finally, the most elaborate customer validation session we've been a part of took place when a client invited a dozen senior executives from target prospects and customers to an offsite event that was organized to provide some continuing education, but a good share of it was to have the attendees review and comment on the company's new customer messaging content.

The result was worth the effort as the company established a new level of rapport with key industry leaders, who literally helped shape and put the finishing touches on the messaging. This creates a unique partnership bond, while ensuring the new messaging will resonate as it's deployed throughout the rest of the marketplace.

Key Chapter Take-Aways

- A **Cross-Functional Messaging Workshop** includes people from sales, services, technical support, marketing, or others who constitute the "dream team" that you wish you had with you when selling to a specific industry or buyer type.
- The **CMM Conversation Roadmap** guides content creation and includes the messaging components for copywriting.
- **Content Validation** ensures that the messages resonate with both sales and customers.

- As the message writer, use your "**Who Cares?**" measuring stick often. If you are writing something that you could not credibly say to a customer, the odds are that salespeople won't say it either, and customers won't believe it.
- Don't fill content boxes just to fill in content. If you feel like you're writing "**fluff**" or making up the story, go back to your "A" players to get more input. Better to get it right than lose credibility with fluff.
- Work hard on the **value points.** "Optimize," "minimize," "maximize," and "improve" don't mean a lot to a customer who is trying to achieve (and measure) achievement of a specific goal. Be as tangible, measurable, and practical in value creation as possible.

CHAPTER 10

SALES-CYCLE-RELEVANT DELIVERABLE DESIGN

We've mentioned the statistic that nearly 90 percent of collateral created in the name of sales support goes unused in the field. And we've used the term "Collateral" with a big "C"—meaning all of the communications tools and programs we create in the name of sales support.

To this point in the book, we've been dealing with one-half of the reason for this problem: Existing messaging doesn't reflect the conversations that you want salespeople to have with customers. Salespeople don't find product-focused content as helpful when they are trying to conduct customer-focused sales calls.

The second half of the equation is equally important: The content doesn't work the way salespeople work. A sales cycle typically consists of iterative steps and communications that document the progression of a deal. If you were to do an assessment to find out when most of your existing collaterals are used, you'd likely find three things:

1. Sales isn't aware of most of the material that exists.
2. The tools they use are typically delivered early in a cycle to establish credibility or as an addendum stuck in the back of a presentation folder.
3. There's a whole set of communications—letters, presentations, executive proposals, and customized collateral (you know that your salespeople use *Microsoft Publisher* or other software to create their own brochures)—that do the heavy lifting in a sales cycle.

The last category of communications is what we call "clandestine collateral" and "maverick messages" created by the field without the aid of marketing. You've probably seen copies of these back-door materials circulating in the field and eventually finding their way back to headquarters.

While you might cringe at the quality of the design—or the accuracy of the content, or the inconsistency of the brand—take a deep breath and look at what's really going on. Why were the documents created? Who received them? When were they used in the selling process? How did the documents help move the customer buying cycle forward faster? You can learn a lot about the needs of salespeople by analyzing both the conversations and the collaterals that they use to facilitate and expedite a customer buying decision.

Two conclusions that you may find upon further review of your company's clandestine collateral:

1. There's a lot of messaging in this field-generated collateral, which means that marketing can have a greater impact on sales activities if we can just get our arms around it.

2. There's a clear, repeatable pattern to the most popular field-generated deliverables, which means we can document, design, and produce a next-generation collateral hierarchy that goes deeper into the sales cycle.

The process that we'll use to discover, document, and mirror your company's sales collateral is called *sales-cycle-relevant deliverable design* (Figure 10-1). There are different approaches, but typically we start with an exercise to determine and design the most appropriate and useful marketing communications, training, coaching, and sales support tools.

Figure 10-1

Sales-Cycle-Relevant Communications

Find an Opportunity	Identify the Needs	Develop a Solution	Create a Value Proposal	Negotiate and Close
Set up meeting with a decision maker; prepare yourself for the right level conversation	Identify business issues that the customer is willing to invest ($) in solving; talk to influencers	Map your "best answer" capabilities to the business issues to keep the sale focused and on track	Present measurable value and proof specific to how your solution solves the identified business issues	Propose a clear vision of the solution, cost, implementation, and metrics

↓   ↓   ↓   ↓   ↓

Map the messaging requirements for your sales cycle:

1. Key conversations at each step
2. Tools used before, during, or after
3. Purpose of each tool in terms of progressing the sales cycle
4. The "anatomy" of each tool
5. The ideal selling toolkit to support conversations using your Customer Messaging content

---

The key is to understand the ideal customer buying process and related steps of the sales cycle, and then determine the key applications for CMM content support, including the literal "anatomy" of the most appropriate deliverables and the precise messaging to be leveraged from the CMM Conversation Roadmap to make it go:

- **Map the customer buying process and best-practice sales cycle** (Figure 10-2). This is a facilitated discussion with sales leaders and trainers, as well as the CMM project team. For each step in the cycle you will identify the objectives for each key "meaningful interaction" where a salesperson has a particular conversation or presentation with a customer, and/or needs to provide a specific type of document that advances the process toward a close. In each case, you will identify the specific content and structure of each conversation and deliverable.
- **Construct the coaching and collateral hierarchy.** The same joint sales and marketing participants will determine the tools, types, and variations required to build a library of conversation, presentation, and documentation templates. This includes designing the layout of the tools, the content to be used, graphics required, and other related detail.

Figure 10-2

Diagram the Ideal Customer Buying Process				
Step One	**Step Two**	**Step Three**	**Step Four**	**Step Five**
Who is doing what?	Who is doing what?	Who is doing what?	Who is doing what?	Who is doing what?
To accomplish what?	To accomplish what?	To accomplish what?	To accomplish what?	To accomplish what?
Using what tool, support, or other information?	Using what tool, support, or other information?	Using what tool, support, or other information?	Using what tool, support, or other information?	Using what tool, support, or other information?
Anatomy of the ideal sales-cycle tool:	Anatomy of the ideal sales-cycle tool:	Anatomy of the ideal sales-cycle tool:	Anatomy of the ideal sales-cycle tool:	Anatomy of the ideal sales-cycle tool:
Then map content from Conversation Roadmap to ideal selling toolkit				

What you'll find in this exercise is that salespeople will rarely need or want as much content as marketing usually produces. And that's typically because the customer is looking for someone to provide clarity among the information overload that accompanies a buying decision.

You're also going to find some interesting collateral types that have very specific responsibility for moving a sales cycle forward (Figure 10-3). It's a very rewarding experience to begin seeing how you can intentionally create and deliver collateral that counts in the heat of a sales cycle. The goal of this process is to make this happen on purpose versus by accident.

We sometimes refer to this as a marketing "bill of materials." Much like manufacturers have created a bill of materials that accompanies the product design, development, and manufacturing process—precisely specifying the parts, components, and assemblies required to make their product—we think companies should have a marketing or sales bill of materials. It precisely defines the coaching and customer-facing communications used to help manufacture a successful sales cycle.

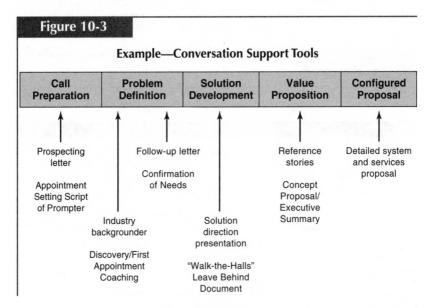

Figure 10-3

Example—Conversation Support Tools

Call Preparation	Problem Definition	Solution Development	Value Proposition	Configured Proposal
Prospecting letter	Follow-up letter		Reference stories	Detailed system and services proposal
Appointment Setting Script of Prompter	Confirmation of Needs		Concept Proposal/ Executive Summary	
	Industry backgrounder	Solution direction presentation		
	Discovery/First Appointment Coaching	"Walk-the-Halls" Leave Behind Document		

Over the past several years of conducting these workshops, the CMM Group has identified several very popular and potent sales-cycle-relevant deliverables. For your consideration, we offer the following examples and descriptions. Later in this chapter we'll show you visual examples, including how the content is leveraged from the CMM Conversation Roadmap:

- **Appointment Setting Letter/Script.** Getting a meeting with the right decision-maker requires the salesperson to quickly hone in on a real business problem, and offer examples and proof points that demonstrate their company's ability to solve the problem.

- **Conversation Talk Track.** Contains all of the messaging components needed to prepare or even conduct a more customer-centered first call or discovery session based on the key business objectives and related pain points identified for a given decision-maker. See example in Figure 10-4.

- **Follow-up Email/Confirmation of Needs and Solution Development.** A template incorporating all of the messaging components needed to respond back to a prospect or customer confirming the findings of the discovery session, proposing a preliminary solution recommendation, and identifying the purpose and participants for the next meeting. See example in Figure 10-5.

- **Preliminary Solution Presentation.** Three *Microsoft PowerPoint* slides summarizing the business need and challenges, along with offering up a possible solution scenario, value proposition, and proof point. All packaged in a highly visual, bullet-point presentation format (with the detail incorporated into the speaker notes). See example in Figure 10-7.

- **Solution Briefs.** A customer-facing, two-page collateral document that leverages your CMM content components to confirm the business objective, proposed solution, potential value, and appropriate proof points. Typically used as an attachment or leave-behind. The content can be designed to look more like an executive summary of a proposal and/or a more customer-needs-centric collateral output. See example in Figure 10-6.

- **Case Study.** A one-page summary of a relevant customer testimonial linked specifically to the identified customer business need and presenting a high-level description of the solution and resulting value.

- **Concept Proposal.** A proactively developed executive-level proposal that describes the possible solution scenario—based on their business needs and our aligned capabilities. It provides the level of detail an internal sponsor can use to bring all of the right parties to the table to gain commitment for a project or to provide resources needed to do a detailed assessment that enables the creation of a final, configured proposal.

After you have identified the sales-coaching and customer-facing tools that align with your sales cycle, the next step is to methodically use your

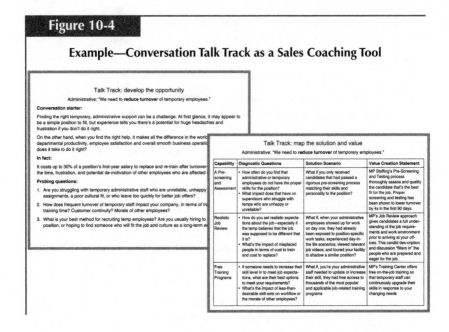

Figure 10-4

Example—Conversation Talk Track as a Sales Coaching Tool

CMM Roadmap content to build those collaterals. Here's where it really gets exciting. All of the content contained in your CMM Conversation Roadmap can be leveraged across all of these new collaterals. So at this step you literally map the pieces of the roadmap that will be used in the various designs—identifying precisely which content will be located where.

In the following examples we've put together samples of the new sales-cycle-relevant collaterals and annotated the specific copy components that have been leveraged from the CMM Roadmap.

Deployment of the new tools and collaterals is the next important step. To determine the optimal implementation and access strategy, you need to coordinate with the marketing and CMM project team, content management resources, and necessary IT contacts to determine a useful content delivery strategy, including how the content is stored, maintained, and made accessible to salespeople in a way that works the way they work.

Here's the challenge: We can build better messaging and even create better sales tools, but if we simply post to our current intranet, our salespeople may never find these materials no matter how good they are. Our deployment strategy has to be equally well thought out and executed to ensure maximum adoption and utility of the CMM approach.

In the next segment of the book (Chapters 11 and 12), we will look at how important sales training and enabling technologies are to successfully

Figure 10-5

Example—Follow-Up E-mail / Confirmation of Needs

Subject: Reducing Turnover in Temporary Administrative Staffing	**Business Issue**
Thanks for an excellent discussion today. This email is to document our conversation and serve as the set-up for our presentation on [insert date] with [participants].	
It's clear that [company] sees an opportunity to decrease costs and improve productivity by reducing turnover in temporary administrative staffing. The biggest challenges we identified include	
➤ Unreliable temporary staff attendance ➤ Dissatisfaction among temporary staff with their assignments ➤ Inability to upgrade skills of temporary staff to meet changing job demands ➤ Poor compensation causing temp staff to leave too soon for better opportunities	**Challenges**
As we discussed, frequent, unwanted turnover is costly and frustrating for everyone involved. The best way to solve this problem is by addressing the root causes of temporary staff turnover. MP Staffing has developed a comprehensive approach, including	**Potential Impact**
➤ *Pre-Screening and Testing* that matches candidate skills and personality with the position ➤ *Realistic Job Reviews* that "filter in" candidates who are qualified, ready, and eager for the job ➤ *Free Training* gives people a way to upgrade skills, stay current, and increase their value	**Solution**
Using a similar solution from MP Staffing, ABC Global dramatically reduced turnover of call center staff from 75% down to 5%. We look forward to working with you on a solution for reducing turnover.	**Proof Point**

launching a CMM initiative. Making sure you engage salespeople in the new messaging and collaterals is essential to institutionalizing the desired approach, and so is the application of appropriate online technologies designed specifically to improve access and utility of sales tools and collaterals.

Meanwhile, for our sales-cycle-relevant deliverable design discussion, we want to first establish the key principles for deployment. The CSO Insights study discussed earlier in the book, along with a survey we conducted with

Figure 10-6

Example—Solution Brief as Customer Leave Behind

How can we reduce unwanted turnover in administrative staff?

MP Staffing Administrative Solution

Figure 10-7

Example—Value-Selling Presentation as Solution Summary

Proof point to validate the business case

Reducing Turnover at ABC Global

ABC Global dramatically reduced turnover among temporary staff in the call center **from 75% to 5%**, by working with MP Staffing.

The business issue:
Unwanted turnover is costly and frustrates everyone who has t[o]

[company name] is struggling with temporary staff that is:

☐ unreliable in their attendance
☐ unhappy with their assignments
☐ a poor fit with corporate culture
☐ Leave too soon for "better offers"

In fact:
It costs up to 30% of a position's first-year salary to re[place] after turnover–not including the time, frustration, and motivation of other employees who are affected by th[is]

How MP Staffing can help you solve the problem

MP Staffing assumes the burden of finding candidates with the right fit, commitment, and skill sets necessary to pick up and stick with the job.

 Pre-Screening and Testing

▶ *Pre-Screening and Testing* matches skills and personalities with the position and company culture

 Realistic Job Reviews

▶ *Realistic Job Reviews* "filter in" the bestcandidates based on your job specifications and industry

 Free Training

▶ *Free Training* gives people a way to upgrade their skills, keep current, and increase their value

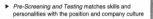
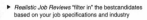

Figure 10-8

Portal—What Are You Selling Today?

CUSTOMER MESSAGING TOOLKIT	
What market are you selling to today?	

Administrative	This toolkit maps the key conversations that our salespeople have with customers, and the sales tools used to develop opportunities.
Engineering	
Manufacturing	
Financial Services	Use the messages and sales tools to prepare for calls, follow up with customers, and position MP Staffing as a company that understands and solves problems.
Education	
Healthcare	
Retail	To get started, choose a market on the left, and then follow the prompts to create a customized sales toolkit.
Call Center	
Accounting	
Daycare	Good Selling!

---

the CMO Council, described the keys to more successful delivery of marketing content:

1. Single, centralized online access point
2. Sales opportunity or customer scenario-based search approach
3. Customizable, configurable content staged to the sales cycle

The following example isn't meant to be the ultimate interface design, but is rather to give you a sense of these principles, and give you something to reflect on as you think of the salesperson's experience at your company as they search your current intranet for help.

What are you selling today (Figure 10-8)? Establish a content-filtering process based on what the salesperson is trying to accomplish as part of a specific sales opportunity. They know their opportunity better than they know the depth and breadth of your company offering and intranet content.

What specific needs have you identified (Figure 10-9)? Either in prep or after an initial conversation, this step in the filtering process

---

Figure 10-9

Portal—What Needs did You Identify?

CUSTOMER MESSAGING TOOLKIT

What market are you selling to today?

Administrative	
Engineering	
Manufacturing	
Financial Services	
Education	
Healthcare	
Retail	
Call Center	
Accounting	
Daycare	

Conversation Roadmap: Administrative

Click on any business issue below to get the full story. Think of these issues as the triggers for the conversations that you have with buyers in this market.

Directors of Administrative and Support Services need to

Improve the quality of candidates for temporary positions
Reduce turnover of temporary staff
Provide quicker placement ("fill rate")
Speed ramp-up and productivity
Improve temporary staffing process management
Manage cost of temporary staffing support
Enable staffing vendor consolidation to save money

---

helps salespeople begin to shape a sales cycle based on customer needs instead of starting with company products. Here you see the top identified customer business needs from the CMM exercise.

Online coaching and confirmation (Figure 10-10). Immediately the salesperson is presented with a sales-ready summary of the company's best response to a select business need. They can click one level deeper to get more detail if desired. The content for these web pages is lifted directly from the CMM Conversation Roadmap. It provides a just-in-time coaching opportunity, as well as a preview of the messaging that's contained in the available sales tools.

Opportunity-specific sales tools (Figure 10-11). At this point, the salesperson is guided to pick the needed coaching and/or customer-facing communications tools—related to the chosen business need—all within a very simple, single experience on your intranet site. This also is where you can help reinforce the preferred sales process by aligning the specific tools with the identified stage of the sales cycle. This can be

---

Figure 10-10

Portal—Is the Customer Interested in Solving the Problem?

CUSTOMER MESSAGING TOOLKIT

Conversation Starter:

We need to **"reduce turnover of temporary staff"**

Related challenges:
- Getting temporaries that are not a good fit with the assignment or the culture
- Temporary staff doesn't have a broad enough skill set to flex with the job requirements
- Temporaries are too easily lured away before finishing the job

In fact:
- It costs up to 30% of a position's first-year salary to replace and re-train after turnover—not including the time, frustration, and potential de-motivation of other employees who are affected by the turnover.

Probing questions:
- Are you struggling with temporary administrative staff who are unreliable, unhappy with their assignments, a poor cultural fit, or who leave too quickly for better job offers?
- How does frequent turnover of temporary staff impact your company, in terms of training and re-training time? Customer continuity? Morale of other employees?
- What is your best method for recruiting temp employees? Are you usually hiring to fill a temporary position, or hoping to find someone who will fit the job and culture as a long-term employee?

Proof:

At ABC Global, MP Staffing reduced turnover from 75% to 5% in the call center.

What do you need to do today?

DOWNLOAD your selling kit for this business issue:

- ❏ Conversation starter
- ❏ One-minute message
- ❏ Appointment-setting script
- ❏ Sales call Talk Track
- ❏ Follow-up letter
- ❏ Solution Brief
- ❏ Presentation slides
- ❏ Case Study
- ❏ Proposal content

---

much more sophisticated than the example, but the key is consistently linking the messaging, content, and sales process to drive your company's ability to sell solutions.

From here the salesperson is "pushed" (instead of having to "pull") the selected sales–cycle–relevant deliverable containing our new customer–needs–centric messaging. Again, compare this example and outcome to your current sales support experience:

- How much faster will salespeople be able to find what they need?
- How much more quickly will they be able to come up to speed on the desired selling messages for a given opportunity?

Figure 10-11

Portal—What is Our Best Answer Solution?

CUSTOMER MESSAGING TOOLKIT

Solution Map:

We need to **"reduce turnover of temporary staff"**

Pre-screening and Assessment Diagnostic Questions:
- How often do you find that administrative or temporary employees do not have the proper skills for the position?
- What do you do if a temporary person is not a good cultural fit for your work environment?
- What impact does that have on supervisors who struggle with temps who are unhappy or unreliable?

Solution Scenario:
- What if you only received candidates that had passed a rigorous pre-screening process matching their skills and personality to the position?

Value Creation Statement:
- MP Staffing's Pre-Screening and Testing process thoroughly assess and qualifies the candidate that's the best fit for the job.
- Proper screening and testing has been shown to lower turnover by 4x in the first 90 days.

Our solution:
- Pre-screening and Assessment
- Realistic Job Review
- Free Training

What do you need to do today?

DOWNLOAD your selling kit for this business issue:
- ☐ Conversation starter
- ☐ One-minute message
- ☐ Appointment-setting script
- ☐ Sales call Talk Track
- ☐ Follow-up letter
- ☐ Solution Brief
- ☐ Presentation slides
- ☐ Case Study
- ☐ Proposal content

- How much more useful will the tools they receive be in terms of advancing a customer dialogue and sales cycle?
- How much more relevant will marketing support be to the revenue-generating activities of your sales force?
- And finally, what are the chances that your company will increase the consistency and quality of overall sales performance?

In the next section of the book, we will expand on the deployment of a CMM initiative. We'll look at how this approach changes everything about sales training; we'll examine the potential for today's technology to take it across the enterprise; and we'll share more specific examples and case studies.

Key Chapter Take-Aways

- The first reason that messaging and collaterals are unused by sales is that they don't **mirror the real-world conversations** that sales has with customers. The second reason is that the marketing deliverables or collaterals don't **map to the sales cycle.** For both of these reasons, sales often develops a whole new set of tools—clandestine collaterals—out of the need to **facilitate and expedite the customer buying process.**

- **Sales-cycle-relevant deliverable design** is a critical step in the CMM process. Use this workshop time to map the sales process and identify what materials are used with customers (before, during, or after the call), the specific purpose of each document in terms of facilitating the buying process, and the anatomy of the document.

- The content that you developed from the Messaging Workshop—using the Conversation Roadmap—can be parsed out to a variety of document types that support the sales cycle. There's no need to "start from the drawing board" each time a new collateral is requested. By defining the customer-needs-driven content and mapping it to the collateral requirements of the sales process, you have effectively defined the **ideal set of sales-coaching and customer-facing deliverables** for marketing.

SECTION THREE

CMM IN PRACTICE: ENTERPRISE DEPLOYMENT

CHAPTER 11

CMM DELIVERY: ENSURING SALES ADOPTION AND USE

Ultimately, the success of your Customer Message Management initiative will come down to how well you "institutionalize" the messaging and tools across the organization—including far-flung salespeople, distributors, and channel partners.

Sounds like the perfect job for technology, doesn't it? We agree. The problem is that so many companies have put the technology "cart" before the content "horse" that we now see a landscape littered with poor or failed implementations, technology shelf-ware, and what we call *sales tool fatigue.*

We became so enamored with the golly-gee, whiz-bang capabilities of software packages, and how they could help speed up content delivery and access, that we neglected to make sure our content was worthy of all this exposure. Or we failed to monitor the content we put out, and we ended up with what one Fortune 500 salesperson called "a cesspool of information."

Our friend and customer-centric sales guru Mike Bosworth is fond of saying: "If your content sucks, then all automation is going to do is speed up the sucking."

A bit brusque, but it makes the point. Our belief is that if you've read this book, and put the previous principles into practice, you are ready to success-fully leverage all the promise of technology. That's because you will have already done the following:

1. Created more customer-focused messaging
2. Built more sales-ready content and tools
3. Trained salespeople on the new messaging and tools

And you've done it all in a cross-functional approach that engages marketing and sales throughout the process. The technology you choose to deploy your CMM content will now be a seamless extension of the initiative and a natural connection between HQ and the field.

CMM NOTE

> *"The use of consistent sales collateral [via technology] may also help train salespeople and reinforce the most effective ways to present information to prospective clients. New representatives may acquire sales skills by examining successful past proposals directed toward the industries they currently target. In this way, the proposal creation process serves as a form of market intelligence and informs decisions regarding the appearance of future proposals."*[1]

A CMM Technology Buyer's Guide

Over the years, a number of marketing and sales content management technologies have emerged. If you look at any of their Web sites, you'd almost swear they were the same tool. Why? Because each one claims to solve the same business problems, which ultimately helps increase the efficiency and effectiveness of marketing and sales. Most recently, we've heard the term *sales enablement* to describe this category.

We've spent the last couple years reviewing all of the latest so-called sales enablement technologies, and will take the rest of this chapter to provide you with a "Buyer's Guide" to determining which one may be right for you.

Let's start with what's in place today. It's been our experience that most companies have some—or several—of the following technologies already in place:

1. **CRM system.** At least some sort of sales opportunity/contact management system or database that is occasionally linked between sales, marketing, and services. These can be home-grown databases, or packages from major CRM vendors such as Siebel/Oracle, SAP, Salesforce.com, and a host of mid- to small-market CRM software companies.

    It's been our experience that CRM is not meeting the needs of salespeople when it comes to helping them be more successful in their day-to-day conversations with customers. One salesperson from a major manufacturing company put it this way: "My challenge is to convincingly communicate the value and distinction of our offering, and then quickly provide customized follow-up information after

---

[1]Peppers and Rogers, "Software Streamlines Sales-Proposal Process," www.searchcrm.com (November 2002).

the sales call. But there's nothing in our CRM system that helps me do that."

CRM systems focus on asking salespeople to put information in that helps sales management better track and manage sales pipelines and forecasts. There is limited utility for the frontline salesperson looking for support in closing a deal.

2. **Intranet** or similar type online Web site or portal where marketing departments place content and sales comes to find it. This is typically an internal IT project or possibly off-the-shelf software.

   Intranets are usually chock-full of information that marketing believes sales needs to sell better, but as we've said throughout this book, the content is not written or organized in the way that salespeople sell. Typical of the comments we hear is this one from a salesperson at a major software company: "Our Internet is a cesspool of information . . . there's too much of it, and most of it is useless garbage."

   Just because all of your documents are available in digital files and online with 24/7 access—even in a single, central location—does not mean you are meeting the accessibility and utility needs of salespeople.

3. **Content management.** Some companies have adopted content management systems that can range from Web site content management only to an enterprise repository for creating, delivering, storing, and managing documents, content elements, and other digital marketing assets across all departments. Some of the big names here include Interwoven, EMC, and Documentum.

   What we are seeing and hearing in this category is that these systems have been perceived as too big, too expensive, too complex for marketing to leverage as a sales-facing communications repository. It can be effective as an infrastructure system for managing, maintaining, and sharing enterprise content, but it lacks the agility and nuance required to be an interface for marketing to manage as a sales entry point and resource.

4. **Proposal management.** A point solution popular in many companies is some sort of dynamic proposal assembly software. Previously regarded as a tool for a proposal center or team, some companies are buying more licenses and pushing this capability out to the entire field as a sales efficiency strategy.

   As a dynamic document generation tool, these systems can be very useful. They guide salespeople with simple wizards or interviews to make selections that drive custom document creation and delivery. Salespeople get a fast document (letter, proposal, white paper) tailored to the specifications they input. Marketing gets more control over the core content used in the field.

The big limitation is that this becomes an island of automation and dynamic content that needs to be maintained and sales needs to find their way to. What's often missing is a seamless link to other existing, static, stand-alone materials and presentations.

5. **Presentation management.** Another point solution companies have invested in to improve control and centralize accessibility over *Microsoft PowerPoint* presentations. The ubiquity of *PowerPoint* has made it a runaway train when it comes to enforcing consistency, accuracy, and quality.

By offering a single point of management, companies have been hoping to give value to sales while regaining some oversight. We've seen some interesting and effective tools in this category, including audio-annotated slides that give salespeople just-in-time coaching from subject matter experts or best presenters. In some cases, *PowerPoint* has become the voice of the sales cycle, while in others it is rarely used and not recommended. Either way, it too can become an island of automation with separate content that has to be maintained and no connection or consistency back to all of the other support tools and messaging.

You can see what's happening here . . . an unprecedented proliferation of tools. Add to this the fact that salespeople are creating their own databases to communicate their "tribal knowledge" such as competitive intelligence, references, sales tips, objection handlers, etc. And, sales training companies are adding software to their offering in hopes of making their training more "sticky" after salespeople leave the classroom.

We had the experience where one of the top reps at a major technology company showed us his computer and pointed out that he had 64 databases open on his desktop, each representing a different source he has to go to in order to create consultative responses to customers.

The Total CMM Technology Solution?

The technologies we just described weren't designed to be a total CMM delivery solution. In fact, Customer Message Management is a process-driven solution, not a technology-driven solution. That is the way it should be. Done right, technology is the enablement of excellent process.

However, we realize many of you—after reading this book—may be wondering what a total integrated CMM technology solution looks like. After all, if you build better messaging and tools, and even train on it, you still need to deliver the content in a way that meets the just-in-time, opportunity-specific learning style we've mentioned before.

So, what's needed to most effectively integrate this CMM messaging and content with the field in a way they will use it?

To help you out, we've established six key criteria for a CMM technology deployment, as identified by extensive surveys done by the CMM Forum, as well as information gleaned from surveys completed by the CMO Council and CSO Insights. (See Figure 11-1 for a summarized list of criteria.) Consider this your "buyers guide" or shopping checklist when you're deciding on CMM enablement solutions:

1. **Centralized, single repository for sales information.**
   Salespeople would always prefer one place to go for the information they need, and ideally it should have a seamless link with their CRM/opportunity management system. This means a single, online location with single sign-on and true back-and-forth sharing of content to personalize the documentation without re-entering data, and to store the content used for a customer in one opportunity file.

2. **Intuitive interface options.** The system should have the flexibility to allow salespeople access to messaging and content based on the way they want to get it ("what do you need to do today?"). This typically includes a simple wizard or "situational" interview approach that allows a salesperson to describe their opportunity, and then the system guides them to the right support messaging and tools. In addition, it will include more straightforward browser search options that allow them to simply track down content. Ideally, it would also include a keyword search function that, like an Internet search engine, would browse all the content and return prioritized recommendations.

3. **Best-practices sharing and reinforcement.** While it's impossible to clone your best salespeople, a system should be able to support and reinforce the company's preferred sales process, as well as facilitate coaching and the sharing of experiences and insights. The key is providing the content in the rhythm of a sales cycle. Your system should give you the ability to parse this content into the right

format and quantity required for key meaningful interactions. It should also support the ability to push rich media components such as audio-annotated slides. And salespeople should be able to search for it in the context of what they are trying to accomplish at that point in the sales cycle. It also gives you an opportunity to reinforce the desired sales training and sales process by making it an inherent part of your content organization and delivery strategy.

4. **Customized, tailored dynamic content creation.** Generic, static content just doesn't cut it in a consultative sales cycle, so you need to enable salespeople to easily personalize outputs for their prospect or customer opportunity. Just putting all of your materials on a portal and creating a better search mechanism isn't going to cut it. The voice of the sales cycle is often *Microsoft Office*—not *Quark Express*. Salespeople need to be able to personalize and tailor their communications and deliverables based on the prospect, customer, and situation. Customers have come to expect a one-to-one experience. If you can't enable this functionality, you have not fully implemented Customer Message Management.

5. **Online community.** The ability to quickly set up private portals for prospects and customers, without IT intervention, eliminates the issue of where email and attachments get lost in someone's inbox or hard drive. As team selling and team buying continues to expand, it also creates a tremendous opportunity for online interaction and community around a specific deal. This reinforces key tenets of the CMM approach. Ideally, the portals you set up should, whenever possible, leverage content from a single database, so if updates need to be made, the content on the portals would be automatically updated as well. Marketers should be able to leverage the portals to maintain consistent contact with specified requested content. And the portals should be so easy to initiate that salespeople are comfortable creating and deploying them without HQ intervention.

6. **Built-in feedback and analytics.** Knowing which messaging and content is being used, how often, when, and with whom, along with providing a very easy path for the field to provide feedback is critical to ensuring your content is hitting the mark and delivering value. Our favorites are the systems that track sales activity as they browse and use the messaging and tools on the system. This provides you with that elusive usage information that can be so important to finding out what works and doesn't . . . and directs your conversations with the field on

how to better help them. Ideally, you will also be able to see what they have actually done in a sales cycle versus counting on them to tell you or manually enter it into an opportunity. If certain activities such as creating a "champion letter" or "sharing a case study" are recommended for a step in the sales cycle, you'll have visibility through the system to see if they've actually used those items. And, finally, it should incorporate a very simple, directed feedback mechanism that allows salespeople to quickly comment and get that information into the system or content administrator.

Figure 11-1

CMM Technology Scorecard

	Low CMM Enablement			High CMM Enablement	
Rate the vendor:	1	2	3	4	5
Single, Centralized Repository: one place for sales to get all necessary sales messages and tools	Online, static library marketing materials available in a digital format			Integrated marketing content repository and sales CRM system that enables single sign-on and true content sharing in a master client opportunity record	
Rate the vendor:	1	2	3	4	5
Intuitive Interface Options: Access strategy that provides content to sales based on the way they want to get it	Global search functionality and drop down menus with structured taxonomy			Online "situational interview" that enables sales to describe needs and system automatically filters messages and *pushes* most appropriate content	
Rate the vendor:	1	2	3	4	5
Best practices sharing: reinforce sales process and facilitate coaching and sharing of experiences and insights	Content is organized and presented to the field by steps in the sales process			Content is enhanced with just-in-time SME coaching information, including audio and video annotation, along with rated, field-supplied insights	
Rate the vendor:	1	2	3	4	5
Content Customization: ability to tailor messages and collaterals based on customer-specific information	Limited customization such as customer and company name, date, logo, and similar, minor inputs			Dynamically generate customized collaterals, presentations, and other documents—on demand—based on sales inputs and selections.	
Rate the vendor:	1	2	3	4	5
Online Community: creating an effective environment for sharing and managing content with prospects and clients	Content is downloaded to sales person's hard drive and shared with customers as email attachment or hardcopy leave-behind			Content is developed and distributed to private portal Web sites that provide the company, prospects, and clients 24/7, updated access to all the opportunity-related documentation and dialogue	
Rate the vendor:	1	2	3	4	5
Built-in feedback and analytics: analysis of content usage patterns and easy feedback for sales users	Analytics to determine marketing Web site hits, document views, and downloads			Sales person-by-sales person and opportunity-specific tracking of messaging and tool use, along with instant email feedback opportunity throughout user experience	

These are some of the companies we are familiar with that address one or more of the six CMM Enablement criteria we just described. Depending on your most pressing needs, different systems provide different capabilities. In many cases, some of the point players can complement other point players to help create a seamless solution. We've tried to identify the areas, as we best understand it, that each company can contribute in.

Key Chapter Take-Aways

- Reasons for **marketing and sales technology failures:** sales tool fatigue, putting the technology cart before the content horse, and buying "shelfware" that is never implemented because of lack of support, lack of funding, or bad product selection.
- **Technology options** vary from CRM systems to intranets, content management, proposal management, presentation management, and a variety of internal databases.

Customer Message Management is a **process-driven solution,** not a technology-driven solution—which is the way it should be. In this chapter we outlined six recommended criteria for evaluating CMM technology options.

CHAPTER 12

CMM TURNS COMMODITIES INTO SOLUTIONS

One of the biggest messaging and selling challenges today is avoiding parity in our value propositions, which can lead to commoditization by our customers. How do you avoid the commodity trap—selling your products and services based on their features and specifications—and differentiating on price? It's not easy.

End customers or buyers tell us that they're not interested in products—and that we're in the era of "overchoice" where everything looks and sounds the same, so there really is no choice anymore.[1] A recent survey[2] of purchasing agents asked the question: "How can vendors sell value to you?"

The response: "They can't."

That was the nearly unanimous response from people who are trained to ignore our pleas regarding differentiation and value. Theirs is a cold, cruel, calculating, number-crunching world.

So the question was reframed. "How can vendors sell value to your company?" This time the answer was different. "Find a business manager who cares, and convince them that you uniquely solve their business issue—in a way they are willing to defend with me."

"So You're Saying I Have a Chance?"

You have a chance of distinguishing yourself even if your company sells something perceived at parity with the competition. To help you do this on purpose, instead of by accident, we've come up with a way to leverage CMM's approach to creating customer-focused selling messages to help your company turn commodities into solutions. We call it *Big Idea Messaging*.

The fact is that ideas are for sale today. The company that gives customers a good idea for solving a problem earns the credibility. They're seen as a valued advisor rather than part of the parade of peddlers.

---

[1] "There is no choice in overchoice," said Alvin Toffler in his book *Future Shock*. He says that an abundance of choice or "overchoice" results in customers being unable to make buying decisions. New York, NY: Bantam Doubleday Dell Publishing Group, June 1984.

[2] Shonka, Mark. *Beyond Selling Value: A Proven Process to Avoid the Vendor Trap*. Chicago, IL: Dearborn Trade, September 2002.

It all starts in the first meeting with a potential business decision-maker. A lot of consultative or solutions-oriented sales trainers and salespeople are convinced that open-ended questions and detailed discovery checklists are the key to successful first meetings. We're here to tell you that's not true anymore, especially as you sell to higher-level buyers. They don't have time for time-consuming small talk.

One Senior Vice President (SVP) decision-maker recently said, "If you plan to come in here and play 20 questions, forget it. I'm looking for big ideas. If I'm going to give you 15 minutes, you better have some relevant insight into how I can do something better or it ain't happenin'!"

That wasn't the only time we've heard this feedback from executive and senior management decision-makers. In many of our recent messaging workshops we're told these potential prospects will kick you out nearly immediately if you begin to pepper them with a checklist of open-ended questions.

Consider a "Big Idea" Conversation

We set out to see if we could codify the contents of the "big idea" conversation as identified by senior buyers, in hopes of finding a cure for the commodity sales call.

What we found is that a Big Idea conversation is still guided by questions—because questions focus the discussion and make sure the customer is doing what they want to do—buy. But these questions need to be framed in a way that enables the salesperson to offer continual value-added insights—and create responses that help confirm a business problem and begin to create a solution.

To help you understand this concept, here's a simple example of Big Idea Messaging in a conversational format (Figure 12-1). After you read it, we'll diagram the content creation process that went into it:

Situation. We are a perceived commodity wholesaler providing medical supplies and pharmaceuticals to healthcare systems, hospitals, and other providers.

Key decision-maker. Our salesperson is calling on a hospital executive.

Top business imperative. Hospital executive is looking for ways to drive more revenue in market with declining reimbursements.

Big Idea. *We can help you maximize your revenue from medications and supplies.*

Figure 12-1

Big Idea Messaging Prompter

Transition	Trial Statement	Compelling Factoid	Proof Point
• A recent American Hospital Association survey reported that hospitals are considering some non-traditional paths to finding new revenue sources due to declining reimbursements. • *What kinds of new revenue sources are you tapping?*	• One of the opportunities mentioned in the survey was improving medication and supplies cost recovery. • They said there's a significant revenue leak in hospitals, making sure expensive medications and supplies are billed properly, in addition to losses due to indigent care. • *How concerned are you that this is a potential revenue leak at your institution?*	• It's been our experience that less than 25 percent of the hospitals we meet with have focused any attention on this possibility, but those who have tell us they've documented **between a 10–20 percent increase** in revenues from improved medication and supplies billing . . . and a **12–15 percent increase in charity care reimbursement.** • *How significant would these improvements be if you put your real-life numbers in there?*	• In one example, [our company] worked with Acme Healthcare System to **generate $14 million of new income** annually just by increasing charity care reimbursement. • We helped maximize the hospital's ability to take advantage of various patient assistance programs from manufacturers and the government. • Next, we're going to integrate medication and supplies delivery with their clinical information systems to ensure more accurate and effective billing—and the **projected new income is nearly $19 million over the next three years.** • *How could solutions like this help you meet your objective for increasing revenue?*

Can you see how a Big Idea Messaging-based conversation can help a salesperson differentiate your company in a commodity discussion? In this example, there are several competitors who not only do the same thing, distribute drugs and supplies, but actually offer the exact same products from the same manufacturers. So this could quickly degenerate into a "cost of goods" discussion.

However, with the support of Big Idea Messaging, salespeople are equipped to have something other than a price war. In fact, they are now equipped to speak to a business decision-maker—not the purchasing agent—about real-life business issues and how the company can help solve them. And they are equipped to avoid the 20 questions game and offer insight throughout the meeting.

Messaging Up Versus Messaging Down

Too often companies start with their products or programs, and they "message down"—meaning they describe the individual features, how they function, and the proposed benefits they offer. As a result, sales conversations occur down at the component level, not up at the customer imperative level. In a commodity selling situation, chances are that these products—let alone these features—will be virtually indistinguishable from the competition. So be prepared to get hammered by purchasing when you "message down."

In the case of Big Idea Messaging, the ultimate Big Idea may actually be comprised of several products, programs, or services that are very similar to the competition when standing alone. However, when these capabilities are combined in the Big Idea Messaging discussion, you will be "messaging up" in a way that shows how we leverage these capabilities to solve a larger, more pressing business problem.

Let's take a closer look at the Big Idea Messaging template to better understand this concept.

Big Idea Messaging Templates

So where did this content come from to create the Big Idea Messaging example above? The principles come from the Customer Message Management approach, which is designed to help you create more customer-focused—versus company and product-focused—sales messaging.

The Customer Message Management system provides a structured architecture for the typically unstructured process of sales messaging. Companies spend lots of time and effort on corporate brand messaging and even product messaging. But most of its best sales messaging is the result of tribal knowledge, not a purposeful strategic initiative.

This is critical, as we've discussed, because it is often the quality of the sales conversation that determines if a customer will view you as a commodity or solutions provider. The Big Idea Messaging template is one tool within the CMM system designed to help companies turn the sales messaging process into a corporate asset.

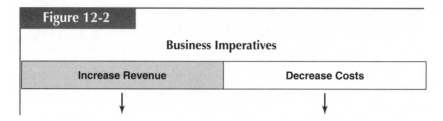

Figure 12-2

Business Imperatives

Increase Revenue	Decrease Costs

Let's look at the anatomy of a Big Idea Messaging template in order to provide you with a tool for identifying and crafting Big Idea Messaging of your own:

Key decision-maker. Choose a targeted decision-maker in a key segment you typically call on.

Top two business imperatives. These are usually the "safe bets" as the top business imperatives for most executive decision-makers, but you can identify others and put them at this level. (See example in Figure 12-2.)

Relevant challenges. Identify the top challenges associated with each business imperative. What problems are keeping targeted decision-makers from achieving the imperative? What untapped opportunities exist to respond to the imperative? (See example in Figure 12-3.)

Solution mapping. Determine what capabilities (products, services, programs) your company can bring to the table to help solve one or more of the listed challenges. At this step you are linking previously disparate activities to create a sense of common purpose aimed at positively impacting the customer's business imperative. (See example in Figure 12-4.)

Big Idea naming. Craft a name that effectively summarizes these mapped capabilities into a descriptive phrase—starting with a verb—

Figure 12-3

Relevant Challenges

#1 [Revenue Challenge]	#1 [Cost Challenge]
#2 [Revenue Challenge]	#2 [Cost Challenge]
#3 [Revenue Challenge]	#3 [Cost Challenge]
#4 [Revenue Challenge]	#4 [Cost Challenge]

Figure 12-4

Solution Mapping

Mapped Relevant Capabilities	Contextual Value Statement
Capability #1 [Key product, service, program, or feature that helps respond to one or more of the challenges]	[How this solves the challenge and responds to the imperative]
Capability #2 [Key product, service, program, or feature that helps respond to one or more of the challenges]	[How this solves the challenge and responds to the imperative]

that explains how you will be helping them solve the challenge(s) and contribute positively to achieving the business imperative.

Big Idea Messaging prompter. Create a conversation support tool that guides salespeople through a logical progression of insights, questions, and possible solutions. (See example in Figure 12-5.)

Figure 12-5

Big Idea Messaging Prompter

Transition	Trial Statement	Compelling Factoid	Proof Point
• Identify a compelling industry statistic or fact that creates a nice transition into your big idea conversation.	• Highlight a possible link between the industry statistic and the big idea you want to talk about.	• Describe your company's experience in dealing with this challenge and the typical results you've generated.	• Share a compelling example of how a customer has succeeded in leveraging the Big Idea.
• Q: Understand their situation.	• Q: Find out if they are dealing with a similar problem.	• Q: Determine if there's interest in the implied Big Idea.	• Q: Ask what kind of value a solution like this could have for them.

What Do Salespeople Say About Big Idea Messaging?

Big Idea Messaging Prompters can guide the salesperson to ask consultative questions while adding value during an executive meeting. In terms of driving sales revenue, this approach helps the rep create a clear vision for how the customer might engage your company to solve a specific problem—with specific results.

We realize that no dialogue between a decision-maker and salesperson will go according to a script or a plan. The Big Idea Messaging approach, however, is often the missing support tool that will increase the odds in your company's favor.

The rubber meets the road in the field, when salespeople actually use the new messaging in customer conversations. So what's the difference when they apply Big Idea Messaging versus traditional product messaging? Here's what several salespeople had to say to one of our clients:

- "I tried it (the Big Idea Messaging) on a recent call with an executive at a big opportunity. The format was easy to follow, so I could actually use the messaging. The messages worked great."

- "The way it flows and allows you to pick the right message template for your customer's needs, and then present possible solutions and real examples from other customers, worked perfectly. . . ."

- "The messaging allowed me to leave the meeting knowing with 100 percent certainty what I was going to have to do to win the business. I confirmed their goals and mapped the solutions—all in the course of one meeting."

- "The messaging helped me show them that we are the growth partner they were looking for."

- "It was a whole different conversation than we normally have. Instead of going in and talking about the cost of goods, we were able to talk about issues and present higher-level solutions."

Your salespeople and sales management know that they need to sell consultatively—developing solutions that deliver bottom-line value. But it's not easy, because everything in their messaging arsenal starts first with the product, not the customer's problem. As marketers, we can change that with Big Idea Messaging.

These sales testimonials are the kind of feedback marketing departments want to get from the field—because then we know that we are increasing our relevance and impact on selling. We're part of revenue-generation.

When you deploy a Big Idea Messaging approach, remember that this content should be leveraged across sales-cycle-relevant tools designed to reinforce a Big Idea conversation. This content needs to be leveraged in sales coaching and customer-facing communications to support a differentiated dialogue that rises above parity-driven product and pricing discussions.

Key Chapter Take-Aways

- **Purchasing agents operate in a cold, cruel, calculating, number-crunching world.** Presenting value requires finding a business manager who believes that your solution solves a business problem and has the potential to provide business value.

- A **Big Idea conversation** positions your capabilities, products, services, and solutions as insights that can impact executive imperatives.

Chapter 13

CMM Fuels the Sales Training Process

When it comes to sales training, how can you move from "checkmark"— just measuring completion—to ensuring "conversational competency"?

Features-based training isn't working. We tell our sales teams to solution sell, yet we train and support them on product-feature-specification. It's a fact of organizational life—most training, marketing communications, and sales tools are built within and for the individual business units. The AMA's CMM Forum has determined that 70–90 percent of the stuff that's created in the name of sales support and sales training is never used by sales. Multiply this by the fact that less than about 10 percent of product training sticks, according to the rule of thumb. The picture is dismal.

Training in product silos usually fails to match the "life and times" of the salesperson—the way they actually position and sell solutions to customers. Too often, sales reps walk away from training feeling that it was a waste of time.

Our goal is to flip the training model on its head: Instead of training on the product and its features, we need to train people to hone in on the business needs of the various buyers in each market segment, then understand the buyers' challenges in trying to meet those needs, and finally position the best-answer solution for each need.

In the past year we've noticed an interesting trend in sales organizations— people are getting back to "blocking and tackling" when it comes to the sales process. But it's not about negotiating styles, closing techniques, and other traditional fundamentals. It's about simplification—bringing clarity to the sales process, so it is focused on the customer conversation, the messages, and the tools that really move a sales cyle.

Simplification is the key. We've spent a decade putting faith in sales and customer information systems, and several more decades in sales training. Now we're wondering how to make sense of it all. As a result, three things really need to be dealt with in the area of sales operations and training:

1) What do salespeople really "need to do" to help facilitate a consultative customer buying decision?

2) How are we training them to elevate from transactional product salespeople to solutions and value-oriented customer advisors?

3) What must marketing do to support both these sales operations and training objectives?

Transforming sales training. This book has spent a lot of time on how to improve sales messaging and tools. Now, we turn our attention to how the CMM approach can help transform sales training to meet senior management demands for a consultative salesforce.

How can we build real-world competency models based on the skills and knowledge needed to facilitate more effective buying decisions? And what does that have to do with customer messaging?

The rest of this chapter addresses challenges faced by companies that want to build a sales competency model and support it with customer-focused training and messaging:

- How do we determine and measure the competencies needed to elevate the selling process in our industry?
- Is it possible to align selling, training, and marketing to drive increased sales performance?
- Can we use the same training and messaging model for our partners/ channel?

What's Holding Us Back?

Sales training is a key platform for product marketing to bring their messages to the field. As product teams, we need to be on the training schedule because it's difficult for us to get concentrated talk-time with sales. Training is also time for other corporate groups to gain "sales mindshare." Unfortunately only less than 10 percent of what any of us teach is retained and used.

What holds us back from improving sales training is the same issue that permeates sales and marketing organizations—a disconnect between processes.

Consider this example: We were recently asked by a prominent, global company to design a competency model for their sales organization, and then align it to product marketing. This sample company offers various component products, software, and services that can be sold separately or bundled as integrated solutions. Each product is owned, supported, and marketed by a different product group.

In this example, sales management will tell you that they have three types of sales—a *transactional sale* (single component or standard bundle), a *solution sale* (solution based on specific customer needs or requirements), and a *strategic sale* (large, long-term relationships with dedicated sales and support resources). The buyers and applications change based on vertical markets, but the technical solution is usually the same. The company is transitioning their geographic, highly transactional sales team to a solutions-style selling organization, supported by a telesales team that will handle transactional deals. The high-end, strategic sales will continue to be handled by their corporate sales team.

What happens with training. The company scheduled training for the new sales team. Each product group prepared training on their products and applications. Each product group was given one day to conduct their training as part of the two-week program.

After the training, the reps went out to the field and continued to do what they had always done—they sold what they knew best to the customers and applications they knew best.

One *customer motto* applies well to this situation: "Sell transactionally and we will buy transactionally." Customers will talk to you the way you talk to them. The *motto for salespeople in training* is similar: "Train us transactionally and we will sell transactionally."

The fact is that features-based training isn't working. As product marketers we put the sales team in a dilemma—they are trained to identify customer needs and then develop a solution, yet we supply them with marketing tools and training that tout individual product specs. So the best reps do their own thing, and the B-to-C players shop for friendly buyers and try to convince them of their need for a given product.

Training can quickly become a well-intentioned activity that doesn't help sales revenue.

Training Challenges

As companies bring customer focus to training, they will encounter challenges like these:

- Content *experts reside in the product groups,* so all training must rely on them to provide the knowledge for training programs—no one else knows the details.
- Salespeople are *less motivated* to complete training because it's an activity, not something that helps them sell—no time to spend out of the field in non-selling activity.

- Training resources are stuck in an *activity trap*—doing, doing, doing without impact.

- Training is delivered by a variety of people in a variety of ways to the same groups of people—very *difficult for marketing to influence* how sales receives training.

- Existing tools are not leveraged optimally, or disbanded if they don't support the training strategy—*not sure why sales doesn't use the tools that marketing provides.*

- There is no common competency roadmap or learning strategy in place—*no common language* for how and why we decide to train.

- There is *no common deployment* strategy, driven by ROI and business metrics.

- The *performance review process* is not supported by the training strategy—we evaluate job performance and promote people on criteria that differ from how we train.

The fact is that these challenges don't go away. That would be unrealistic. It's more important that we work within the realities of our organizations and make changes to the processes that govern how we work together.

Everyone wants to work smarter by having more relevance and impact to the organization, but without doing more work. Everyone is busy. Good process can make the difference in how we apply our energies toward a common company goal: driving revenue.

A Process for Aligning Marketing, Messaging, and Sales Performance

Your competitive advantage is less in *what* you sell, and more about *how* you sell it. Building a sales performance or competency model, and developing training, are based on the critical interactions that you expect your sales-people to have in the sales process.

One reason why using customer messaging in sales training might be uncomfortable to marketing is that we're swimming in unknown waters. As one of our CMM clients said recently, "I'm fine when you talk about marketing. When you start talking about sales process and how sales thinks, I'm in very unfamiliar territory. I just don't know the answers, even though I've been in this company for 18 years."

We need to understand sales, and talk to them in their terms. Salespeople are just-in-time, opportunity-specific learners. They are coin operated. They get the information they need, when they need it, to move forward with a specific sale—because that's how they make their sales goals ($).

Some people say that salespeople are motivated only by money. This is not true. The best salespeople we know are *motivated by winning*. They hate to lose. In this game, winning means closing the sale and gaining a customer.

Marry those statements with this comment by a successful sales manager: "Salespeople are like water. We will always flow down the path of least resistance to get to the end point."

As we develop performance models, training, and messaging, we have to do three things:

1. Step One: Map the Sales Process
2. Step Two: Link Performance Expectations to the Sales Process
3. Step Three: Create a Training Blueprint

Let's review each step.

Step One: Map the Sales Process

Sales expectations have to be set in the context of the sales process. Your sales process—whether de facto or sanctioned by the company—probably consists of steps like these:

Figure 13-1

Map Performance Expectations to the Sales Cycle

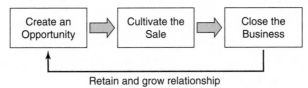

Retain and grow relationship

For each sales position that you will train:

▶ **Define learning objectives**: What are the performance expectations at each step of the customer buying cycle—what do you realistically expect them to DO after the training?

▶ **Determine conversational competency requirements**: Who do we expect them to talk to, about which business issues/pain points, using which coaching/marketing tools or materials?

▶ **Identify "need-to-know" information**: What product information, processes, industry background, company information, systems or applications, research, or other background is necessary as a precursor to the learning objectives and conversational competencies?

How to:

Sales structure. Understand how your sales team is organized in terms of geographies, product responsibilities, roles, reporting structure, compensation plans.

Sales tracking. Ask how sales management tracks sales progress in the pipeline. There may be a percentage associated with each step of the sales cycle that demonstrates progress and is used for forecasting. Also find out how salespeople communicate their sales tracking to management, and if they are expected to submit any completed documents or customer communications to prove their progress.

Sales process. Find out how various salespeople sell to customers— the steps of their de facto sales process (see example on previous page), the customer positions/roles they talk to (influencer/buyer), and what they are trying to achieve at each step.

Sales support. Determine which tools (emails, marketing communications, self-created materials, presentations, product demonstrations, customer testimonials, Web site, technical people, etc.) they use throughout the sales cycle. Ask "is there anything that you usually give or send to the customer at that point? Anyone you involve in the call?" Note that they will usually describe materials that they create themselves. Don't be surprised—they'll be hesitant to tell you what they really use.

Sales Questions

These questions might be helpful as you talk with salespeople about their work:

- What is your current account package? Look for number, types, and sizes of accounts.
- How often do you talk to each account? To the same or multiple people? For what reasons? Look for level and frequency of contact, whether live, phone, or email.
- Who else from our company is in your accounts on a frequent basis? What roles do they play? Look for team roles in supporting the customer, and coordination among roles.
- What percentage of your calls is sales-oriented versus account management? Look for number of selling interactions versus relationship-building interactions.

- Do you have different types of sales cycles—for example, a solution sell versus a component or single-service sale? When do you know that the sale is going to follow a component path versus a solution sell? Do you involve different people in the sale, or speed things up in one case versus the other? Do you have to talk to different buyers depending on the type of sale? Do you get compensated differently for different types of sales? Look for the resources needed in selling different types of offerings.
- How do you track sales activity in your pipeline? Is that required by management? How do you track your progress and next steps? Look for individual systems that are used.
- It helps me understand the sales process if you walk me through a recent "win." Can we discuss a sales cycle starting from how you identified or created the opportunity through close? "What happened next" for each type of sales cycle, who was involved/why, what information was needed, roadblocks that were overcome. Discuss and map it.
- What would change if you were selling [a different type of product]? Can we discuss a similar "win"? Look for variation in sales cycles—solutions, people involved, tools used.

Step Two: Link Performance Expectations to the Sales Process

The goal of this step is to build a competency model in the context of the sales process. This requires us to determine your "conversational" expectations of reps at each step in the sales process. In other words, at each step in the sales cycle, who is talking to whom, about what, to what level of depth?

Why this isn't as easy as it seems   Aligning expectations to the sales process is difficult—because it requires your company to *make decisions about the roles of various salespeople,* channel partners, and support teams. How should various roles collaborate or interact as part of the sales cycle? Should this change over time, as you expect competency levels to increase for selling certain types of solutions or in certain markets? For example, should your "inside sales" team take more responsibility for certain types of sales after you've established your presence in that market, or with those buyers? Are you trying to reduce the cost of sale for certain products by increasing competency among your sales reps and decreasing dependency on specialists?

Another reason why this step is difficult is that *it's not static,* nor should it be. You don't do it once and stop. How you engage your sales channels, and what you expect of them, will change based on the markets you're going after, your company focus, and your offerings. How you train the sales team needs to directly reflect your changing expectations.

How to:

Align sales expectations. For each step of your sales process, what do you expect each sales role to *do*? Start each expectation with a verb. Don't fall back on a checklist of products. You might need to do this for each type of sales cycle.

Group expectations into competencies. Standard sales competencies include things like "Written and Verbal Communication," "Selling Skills," "Financial Acumen," "Industry Knowledge," plus specific technical skills and knowledge—known as "Areas of Expertise." The American Society of Training and Development (ASTD), and a variety of industry books, can provide sample competency models. You should be able to logically group the expectations in a way that makes sense for your company. It doesn't have to follow a predefined model.

Develop a model for competency development. We've provided a sample competency model in Figure 13-2. This model identifies a "hire

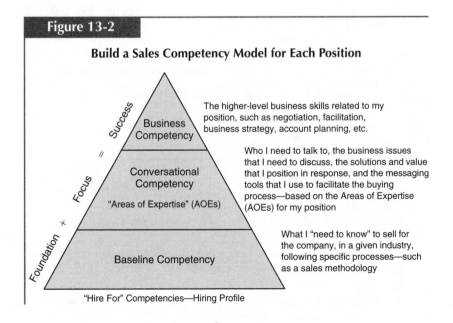

Figure 13-2

Build a Sales Competency Model for Each Position

Success // Focus + Foundation

Business Competency — The higher-level business skills related to my position, such as negotiation, facilitation, business strategy, account planning, etc.

Conversational Competency — "Areas of Expertise" (AOEs) — Who I need to talk to, the business issues that I need to discuss, the solutions and value that I position in response, and the messaging tools that I use to facilitate the buying process—based on the Areas of Expertise (AOEs) for my position

Baseline Competency — What I "need to know" to sell for the company, in a given industry, following specific processes—such as a sales methodology

"Hire For" Competencies—Hiring Profile

for" profile, "baseline" competencies, "areas of expertise," and "business competencies." This is a helpful way to categorize competencies in a way that makes sense to salespeople.

Step Three: Create a Training Blueprint

After you've developed conversational content using the CMM process described in Section Two, and have defined the conversational competencies required at each step of the sales process, the next step is to train salespeople to use the content and tools in mock sales calls.

A training blueprint, or design plan, is your guide for developing the training. It defines the learning objectives, content, and proof (evaluation) that will be required as part of the training session. The difference between Conversational Competency training and typical product training is that the sessions are built around the conversations that your best salespeople have repeatedly and successfully with customers. In other words, the training is built from the customer's perspective, rather than from the company and product perspective. And the "big win" is that your new CMM messaging and sales communications perfectly align with and support those customer conversations. The new messaging and tools become the "fuel" for your sales training.

Figure 13-3

Create a Conversational Competency Training Blueprint

Training goal: Enable sales reps to facilitate the buying process by having the right conversations with key buyers, conveying meaningful and appropriate information to buyers, and positioning the value of our solutions in the context of solving business problems.

Module #	Objective	Content	Proof

To develop the training blueprint:

- **Objectives:** Group learning objectives and conversational competency requirements into modules, and sequence them so that you know which ones are prerequisite to others.

- **Content:** List the information, in-class examples, handouts, tools, or other "need to know" content that will help learners accomplish each objective.

- **Proof:** Determine exactly what you want the learners to demonstrate (via role play, in-class exercise, on-the-job activity, test, etc.) to prove that they are able to DO what the objective stated they should be able to do as a result of the training.

The ultimate test of conversational competency is observing reps in action—creating realistic sales scenarios that require them to practice and demonstrate their ability to conduct key conversations with the types of customers who are most likely to buy from your company. Remember: salespeople are just-in-time, opportunity-specific learners. By delivering training that mirrors their sales conversations and sales cycle, you can reinforce your company's best practices, increase consistency and use of messages, and provide a practical way for marketing to be more relevant to the customer buying process.

Key Chapter Take-Aways

- With the exception of sales skills, **training is behind in terms of customer centricity.** We provide product training, industry overviews, and application knowledge. We leave it to the salesperson to put the story together to address a specific customer need.
- **Training is part of the manufacture of a sale.** It's not a separate, discrete event. It's a key way to help your sales channels gain specific knowledge to target your key markets and sell your solutions.

CHAPTER 14

CMM ACROSS THE MARKETING CONTINUUM

This is the last chapter, but certainly not the least in terms of the broader impact of Customer Message Management on your company. We've discussed the impact of CMM on sales support tools and sales training. Beyond that, however, there needs to be an executive-driven marketing and communications imperative to integrate CMM discipline into these important activities or tools:

- Branding
- Web sites
- Tradeshows
- Advertising
- Direct Marketing
- Public Relations

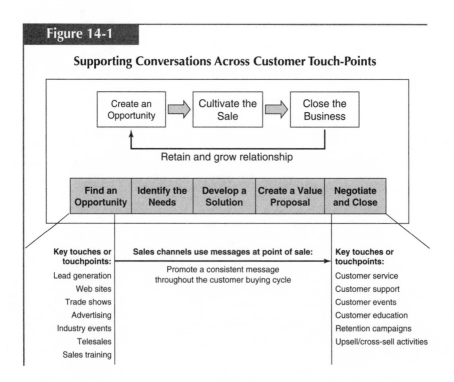

Figure 14-1

Supporting Conversations Across Customer Touch-Points

Create an Opportunity → Cultivate the Sale → Close the Business

Retain and grow relationship

| Find an Opportunity | Identify the Needs | Develop a Solution | Create a Value Proposal | Negotiate and Close |

Key touches or touchpoints:
Lead generation
Web sites
Trade shows
Advertising
Industry events
Telesales
Sales training

Sales channels use messages at point of sale:
Promote a consistent message throughout the customer buying cycle

Key touches or touchpoints:
Customer service
Customer support
Customer events
Customer education
Retention campaigns
Upsell/cross-sell activities

While the CMM process emphasizes the customer conversation and sales-cycle delivery of those customer needs-driven dialogues, the same messages can and should be used across this wider spectrum of integrated marketing communications.

Author Don Schultz comments,[1] "It is important to have an integrated selling line to serve as a basis for every communication discipline. The line should drive the thinking behind every piece of communication. The selling line, stemming from the communication strategy discipline, should significantly differentiate the brand from its competition. It will give a good reason to buy this brand over theirs."

The goal is consistency in presenting your brand, based on what your customers really care about and what they want to accomplish. By using CMM to create customer needs-based messages by industry, buyer type, or solution set, you have built the foundation for a company-wide brand strategy, positioning, and ultimately key messaging that must weave through all other brand communication touch-points.

Your ability to connect corporate branding, marketing, and communications programs with field sales activity goes up exponentially when those programs have their genesis in a messaging approach that makes sense to those that have to represent it in front of the customer. And, it stands a better chance of being used if they've also directly contributed input to the process.

The CMM approach of putting customer problems before company products, and developing a contextual value story that makes sense to the customers, also significantly improves the chances that your prospects and customers will respond to your advertising, direct marketing campaigns, and PR events and programs.

If a buyer prefers salespeople who identify with their business problems and clearly show how the company can help, it stands to reason they'd appreciate corporate marketing interactions that do the same.

However, until the CMM approach documented this customer interaction for marketers, we didn't have a structure to follow or a sense of confidence that we were delivering something customers really cared about or would use. Too many corporate marketing initiatives were the brainchild of really smart headquarters-based executives and creative types, but unfortunately were void of any street-level insight and validation.

Even the customer research and validation that is occasionally performed is often based on reactions to themes and variations of the same

---

[1]Don E. Schultz, *Integrated Marketing Communications,* Lincolnwood, IL: NTC Business Books, 1994, p. 69.

company-centric approaches. While the customers voice their preferences based on what's presented, it doesn't mean these messages would actually move them to action or impact their behavior in a buying cycle.

The CMM approach is the first marketing messaging methodology vetted by salespeople and proven to help facilitate the customer buying process.

While it's early yet, some companies have begun adopting a CMM approach to create corporate marketing messages and materials. Others have started adapting their CMM sales messaging as the foundation for their corporate branding approaches. The following are two examples. The first looks at applying a CMM approach to an integrated branding campaign; the second shows how CMM messaging can be used to re-direct a trade show presence for greater impact.

Case in Point: Staking out a Unique Brand Promise

Many companies invest in brand research to determine their core value proposition in the marketplace. They hold offsite meetings with executives, they host focus groups with prospects and customers, and they try to figure out *if the company was a tree . . . what kind of tree it would be.*

The result of all these efforts usually leads to a set of statements about a company's supposedly unique mission, vision, and position in the market. Thousands, even millions can be spent coming up with this key set of brand positions and messages—often referred to as "pillars." There's only one problem.

When those same companies go to their next trade show or page through their industry trade journals, what do they discover? Their competitors have hijacked those same key messages and words. Darn them.

Well, that's to be expected when companies in competitive markets analyze themselves in the context of who they are and what they bring to market. Because for all intents and purposes, on the surface, the top two or three competitors in any market basically offer the same thing.

As we've discovered in the previous chapters of this book, true differentiation is driven by companies who determine very clearly the key challenges of their customers and have done due diligence in aligning their company assets to those challenges and identified the resulting impact and value they can generate.

It's this grassroots discovery process that yields messages that help articulate competitive differentiation. So it's our contention that these same messages should then be pushed up to the top of the branding, marketing, and communications pyramid to be the basis of your corporate marketing, PR, and demand generation activities. Let's look at some examples.

CMM in a Brand-Building Campaign

Question: How do you differentiate your box that generates an electrical current that creates a spark that heats metal to create a weld that joins two pieces of metal together—from your competitor's box that does the same? Pretty basic stuff, riding the slippery slope of perceived parity.

Answer: Clearly demonstrate how your capabilities can help customers meet a specific business objective and deliver a demonstrable business impact.

In markets where dealers and customers are arguing product parity and price, true brand leaders will elevate themselves to a "solution" by clearly distinguishing their offerings based on how they solve customer problems.

Check out this branding campaign from Miller Electric Mfg. Co., the leading provider of arc welding equipment and supplies. They've created an integrated trade journal online brand advertising campaign that links to a Web site. This is not an unusual approach, until you look at the content. It follows the CMM principles in this book.

At the core of the campaign is a newly created "Results" Web site (www.millerwelds.com/results) (see figure 14-2) that details how Miller

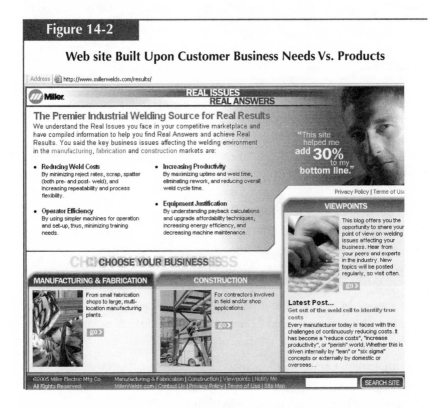

Figure 14-2

Web site Built Upon Customer Business Needs Vs. Products

Electric is helping their customers solve their most critical welding-related business challenges. The challenges were identified and confirmed through customer and distributor research. The corresponding solution stories are real-life customer case studies where Miller combined their various product offerings, services, and process expertise to solve the problem and generate both qualitative and quantitative business impact.

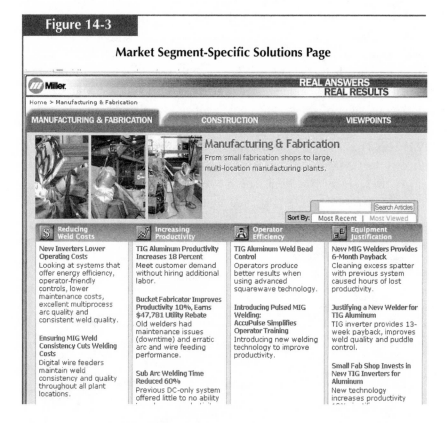

Figure 14-3

Market Segment-Specific Solutions Page

Again, this site is at the center of a brand advertising campaign designed to rise above the "welding box" comparisons and demonstrate Miller's unique ability to understand customer business imperatives and align the company's assets to help meet customer needs.

This is a very different approach from the traditional product, feature-benefit story. Mostly because it starts with the customer profile (key market segments—Manufacturing and Construction), and their realistic business issues:

- Reduce welding costs
- Improve operational productivity
- Respond to lack of qualified welder operators
- Help with new equipment acquisition costs

Employing CMM Principles   Following CMM principles, Miller identified the relevant challenges associated with customer segments and their business imperatives, and then mapped their capabilities to create a best-answer solution. In this case they linked specific examples of how and where they helped meet those challenges for other similar companies.

Miller also ran trade magazine advertisements, Internet banners, and search words promoting the "Results" Web site. The goal was to drive traffic

---

Figure 14-4

Trade Magazine Advertisement to Push Web site Traffic

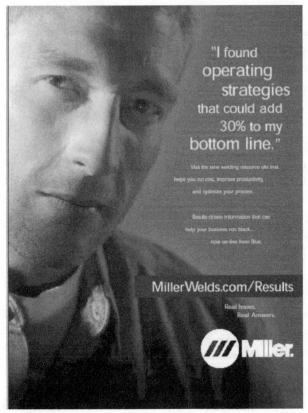

---

and give them a better shot at tracking ROI for their brand advertising spend. The Web site also allows visitors to sign up for email alerts when new value stories are added.

"If companies want to elevate themselves from a 'product' to a 'solutions' provider, they need to do more than just start calling their products solutions," according to Vickie Rhiner, director of marketing communications for Miller. "You have to confirm your customers' key business problems and then make the effort to create messages that show how your company can truly help."

We've seen real-life instances where companies have stopped calling something a product and started to call that same something a solution. Like they waved a magic wand and said . . . "Poof, it is now a solution." Customers will smell this one out. They need to see that you've connected the dots between your company's capabilities and what they need to accomplish before they will consider you a solutions provider.

Case in Point: Differentiating Yourself at Crowded Trade Shows

Think about the last trade show you attended—or produced. How similar or different was the messaging between your company and the competitors' booths? Does anyone really read that stuff anyway?

Your products are there. The panels are up and looking good. The product literature made it on time. The video is working. The floor staff has the right shirts on. But what are we really saying to customers? Are they getting the message? Can they distinguish you in a meaningful way? Are they taking the desired action?

The fact is that trade shows have fallen out of favor as prospecting events, because companies haven't been able to show a significant correlation between attendee numbers and legitimate qualified leads. For the sales team, trade shows are less about generating new leads, and more about entertaining prospects and customers, or engaging them with company executives and experts in an "away-from-the-office" environment.

B2B Magazine notes the fall of Comdex, a premier annual show that "went from king of the trade shows to defunct in about five years' time. PC Expo went through an iteration or two before it disappeared. And once-large, must-attend shows such as Manufacturing Week have become shadows of their former selves."[2]

When a trade show becomes cluttered with similar-sounding presentations, programs, and product demonstrations, how do you differentiate yourself from the competition—in the eyes of your customers? Our answer: *You change the dialogue.*

A trade show is really a series of customer conversations. The company that is able to create, equip, and deliver the most effective conversations

---

[2]*B-to-b marketers have proven remarkably adaptable in the last five years,* btobonline.com, June 13, 2005.

consistently over the course of a trade show stands the best chance of seeing a return on its investment.

Trade Show Conversations at Multiple Levels   Trade show conversations occur at multiple levels—whether customers are reading the message from across the hall, hearing it as part of a group presentation, or engaged in a one-to-one discussion with a representative from your company.

The goal is to drive a consistent message from the booth panels to the conversations with show staff, scheduled presentations, and take-away collaterals. And we think the CMM approach offers you the best chance of separating your company from the traditional product showroom approach of most trade show exhibits.

CMM asks you to critically challenge all of the messaging that goes into your trade show exhibit and assess how well it does the following:

1. Do we demonstrate an understanding of the industry?
2. Do we connect with the key business goals, problems, or needs of the attendee?
3. Do we clearly communicate practical solutions that solve these problems?
4. Can we articulate the business value these solutions provide?
5. How do we prove that we've done it successfully before?

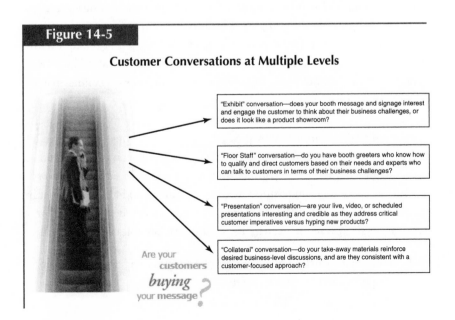

Figure 14-5

Customer Conversations at Multiple Levels

"Exhibit" conversation—does your booth message and signage interest and engage the customer to think about their business challenges, or does it look like a product showroom?

"Floor Staff" conversation—do you have booth greeters who know how to qualify and direct customers based on their needs and experts who can talk to customers in terms of their business challenges?

"Presentation" conversation—are your live, video, or scheduled presentations interesting and credible as they address critical customer imperatives versus hyping new products?

"Collateral" conversation—do your take-away materials reinforce desired business-level discussions, and are they consistent with a customer-focused approach?

Are your customers *buying* your message?

Sound familiar? It should. It's the CMM Message Map that we've used throughout this book. At a trade show, the same messaging approach enables you to engage customers in conversations at multiple levels.

CMM in a Trade Show Setting

Question: How do you break free of and rise above the "cost of goods" discussion when you are a wholesaler that distributes the exact same brands of supplies as your competitor?

Answer: Clearly demonstrate how your operational capabilities, processes, technologies, and services can help customers better meet their business objectives and contribute to the overall mission of their institutions.

One of our CMM clients recently leveraged their CMM project, which was originally established to develop consultative selling messages and customer conversations, and made the new messaging the foundation of their biggest trade show approach.

The result is an integrated go-to-market strategy that links their significant corporate marketing and sales investment in trade shows—with the day-to-day sales messaging and support tools.

Exhibit Messaging   The booth panels and banners begin the conversation with attendees, broadcasting to the crowd that you have something distinct to say. When the attendees enter the booth, this signage became the critical reference point and natural transition for booth greeters to engage the attendee in a discussion regarding their business challenges.

The company dedicated a section of its exhibit to each of the four identified customer business imperatives. Each section was identified by a large hanging banner with the imperative name and a descriptive banner that set up the solution conversation.

Floor Staff Conversation   Obviously, the quality and impact of the exhibit messaging is only as good as the booth staff and their ability to leverage the messaging in their direct conversations at the booth. To ensure that everyone on the show floor understood the new messaging and how to apply it in their customer interactions, CMM helped the company develop a comprehensive pre-show training strategy for each of the key roles:

1. **Concierge staff.** They were booth greeters designated to identify prospects and customers, qualify their interest, and connect them

with a subject matter expert for more a detailed presentation and demonstration.

2. **Subject matter experts.** There were identified experts for each of the four imperatives. They became completely familiar and conversant on the messaging for their section, including the related challenges, the company's relevant solutions and value propositions, and the best customer references.

3. **Product support.** These players provided deep support for specific offerings, including products, services, and programs, and were charged with being able to help customers understand the products within the context of the solution and how it helped respond to the business or clinical imperative.

In the weeks leading up to the show, web training conferences were held to introduce key new messaging, as well as separately scheduled conference calls with each of the key roles to go over their responsibilities.

The day before the show there was a general training session on the new messaging and the booth layout and application. This was followed by break-out training for each of the roles to practice the flow of their conversations, create consistency from section to section in the way the material would be presented, and review the handout support materials. Then, finally, all parties spent time on the show floor to familiarize themselves with the exhibit layout and location of the messaging and support tools.

Feedback regarding this approach to the show was overwhelmingly positive. A survey of key salespeople who participated in the training and on the show floor showed they felt significantly better equipped than previous shows to have a unique conversation with attendees that differentiated them from the competition. And they agreed that the quality of leads and follow-on meetings were vastly improved over previous shows.

Based on this response, the next step for leveraging the CMM messaging is to incorporate it as a foundational element of a complete company re-branding campaign. This makes perfect sense because the heart of any true brand is what the company actually does to help customers do what they need to do.

The CMM approach helps companies define and develop their brand position from the grass roots level up, which gives companies a fighting chance to actually develop a brand campaign that will resonate with the field.

Key Chapter Take-Aways

- While the CMM process emphasizes the customer conversation and sales-cycle delivery of those needs-driven dialogues, the **same messages can and should be used across the wider spectrum** of integrated marketing communications.

- True differentiation is driven by companies who determine very clearly the key challenges of their customers and have done due diligence in **aligning their company assets to those challenges** and identified the resulting impact and value they can generate.

- A **trade show is really a series of customer conversations.** The company that is able to create, equip, and deliver the most effective conversations consistently over the course of a trade show stands the best chance of seeing a return on its investment.

- The goal is to **drive a consistent message** from the booth panels to the conversations with show staff, scheduled presentations, and take-away collaterals.

INDEX

A

activity trap, 153
advisory task force, 117
American Marketing Association,
    2–3, 29
    training programs, 64–65
analytics, 139–140
appointment setting letter/script,
    122–123

B

baseline assessment, 69–70
best-practice sales cycle, 59, 121
best-practices messaging workshop, 101
best-practices sharing and
    reinforcement, 138–139
Big Idea Messaging, 142–149
    conversational format, 143–145
    messaging prompter, 144, 147
    messaging up *vs.* down, 145
    sales testimonials, 148–149
    templates, 145–147
Booz Allen & Hamilton survey, 12
Bosworth, Mike, 134
brand
    communications, 67
    consistency, 161
    decision-making, 12–13
    inconsistent, 41
    loyalty, 12
    positioning, 14, 20
    strategy, sales and service teams
        and, 23
branding
    effect of CMM approach on, 169
    failure of, 16–17
    Miller Electric Mfg. Co. campaign,
        163–166
budget, 10–11
business development, and company
    goals review, 75–76
business goal, 63
business needs, 43, 95–96

aligning capabilities to (solution
    mapping), 39
brand consistency and, 161
challenges (pain points), 33, 35, 95, 97
confirmation of, 123, 125
customer determination of, 35
description, 110
identifying, 38, 83, 120, 127–128
impact if not addressed, 95
sales training and, 150
buyer goals, 73, 74, 95–96
buyer roles, 73, 74, 94–95
buying decisions, customer loyalty
    and, 13
buying process, 131
    mapping, 59, 121
    process alignment and, 8

C

capability value, 97
case study, 123
challenges, 64, 110
channel partners, 7
closing, 120
CMM. *See* Customer Message
    Management
CMM Forum, 150
CMM Group, 2–3
CMO Council, 2–3, 11
coaching, 122
    conversation talk track tool, 124
    hierarchy, 59, 121
    online coaching/confirmation,
        128, 129
collateral, 59
    clandestine, 41, 120
    consistency in, 135
    sales-cycle-relevance of, 30, 119–131
collateral hierarchy, 121
Collins, Jim, 47
Comdex, 166
communication. *See also* collateral
    corporate, 67

171

About CENGAGE LEARNING

Cengage Learning, a progressive and authoritative voice in business publishing, brings to the global business community the expertise and insights of leading thinkers. Our books educate, enlighten, and entertain, and provide an intersection where our authors and our readers share cutting edge ideas, practices, and innovative solutions. Cengage Learning seeks to cultivate, enhance, and disseminate information that illuminates the global business landscape.

www.cengage.com

About the typeface

This book was set in 10.5 point Bembo. Bembo was cut by Francesco Griffo for the Venitian printer Aldus Manutius to publish in 1495 *De Aetna* by Cardinal Pietro Bembo. Stanley Morison supervised the design of Bembo for the Monotype Corporation in 1929. The Bembo is a readable and classical typeface because of its well-proportioned letterforms, functional serifs, and lack of peculiarities.

Library of Congress Cataloging-in-Publication Data

Riesterer, Tim.
  Customer message management : increasing marketing's impact on selling / Tim Riesterer, Diane Emo.
    p. cm.
  ISBN-13:978-0-324-31316-1
  ISBN-10: 0-324-31316-0
  1. Sales promotion. 2. Communication in marketing. 3. Value added.
I. Emo, Diane. II. Title.
HF5438.5.R545 2006
658.8′2—dc22   2006016725